TECHNOLOGY AND SOCIAL POWER

Also by Graeme Kirkpatrick:

Critical Technology: A Social Theory of Personal Computing, 2004
Winner of the 2005 Philip Abrams Memorial Prize, British Sociological
Association

Technology and Social Power

Graeme Kirkpatrick

University of Manchester

First published 2008 by
PALGRAVE MACMILLAN
Houndmills, Basingstoke, Hampshire RG21 6XS and
175 Fifth Avenue, New York, N.Y. 10010
Companies and representatives throughout the world

PALGRAVE MACMILLAN is the global academic imprint of the Palgrave Macmillan division of St. Martin's Press, LLC and of Palgrave Macmillan Ltd. Macmillan® is a registered trademark in the United States, United Kingdom and other countries. Palgrave is a registered trademark in the European Union and other countries.

ISBN-13: 978–1–4039–4728–4 hardback
ISBN-10: 1–4039–4728–7 hardback
ISBN-13: 978–1–4039–4730–7 paperback
ISBN-10: 1–4039–4730–9 paperback

This book is printed on paper suitable for recycling and made from fully managed and sustained forest sources. Logging, pulping and manufacturing processes are expected to conform to the environmental regulations of the country of origin.

A catalogue record for this book is available from the British Library.

A catalog record for this book is available from the Library of Congress.

10   9   8   7   6   5   4   3   2   1
17   16   15   14   13   12   11   10   09   08

Printed in China

To the memory of Annabelle MacKinlay (1916–2006)

Contents

Acknowledgements

This book could not have been written without the help and encouragement of many people. I am fortunate to work in the sociology subject area of the University of Manchester, and have benefited from the support of all my colleagues there. I am particularly grateful to Fiona Devine, Mike Savage, Nick Crossley and Nick Thoburn, who all helped my work on this project by generously sharing their time, ideas and encouragement. Freyja Peters helped protect me from administrative duties when they threatened to derail the writing process in Summer 2006, for which I am very grateful. Joanne Chesters and Ann Cronley were always similarly supportive. I must also thank Catherine Gray, Emily Salz, Sheree Keep and Anna Reeve of Palgrave for their patience and support throughout the writing process and two anonymous reviewers for Palgrave who provided several helpful suggestions. Friends and colleagues at other universities, and some with no institutional affiliation, helped in various ways at different times and so I am grateful to Andrew Feenberg, Helen Kennedy, Jon Dovey, Natalia Hanley, Sarah-Jane Bey-el-Araby, Beverley Skeggs, James Sumner, Piotr Sitarski, Lisa Adkins, Bo Kampmann Walther, Andrew McCulloch and John Wilson. I must also thank students on my third year module, "Technology and Society" (2004–6) for many stimulating discussions of issues I've written about in the book. All the remaining faults with the book are down to me.

Special thanks to Theodor Araby-Kirkpatrick for his unique perspective on digital technology and culture and much else besides. Sarah Carling was a source of ideas, inspiration and companionship throughout the time it has taken me to write this book and I thank her too. This book is dedicated to the memory of my grandmother, Annabelle MacKinlay, who died while it was being written. She was a socialist feminist who combined activism with ingenuity and humour in the face of adversity. She and other working-class people of her generation made it possible that I should be in the fortunate position of writing books.

Technology and Social Power

This book introduces contemporary thinking on the relationship between technology and society, with a particular emphasis on the place of technology in social theory. It is necessarily selective, since the relevant literature is large and the book is quite short. Ideas from the philosophy of technology are discussed, alongside theories and examples from sociology. There is a particular focus on ideas from the Marxist and critical theory traditions, but work from feminist and social constructionist perspectives is also considered. A range of examples are used to highlight particular issues, from calendars and clocks to mobile phones and Fab Labs. In the course of describing the ideas that are covered, I have also made specific criticisms. My hope is that these add up to a position on the relationship between society and technology that synthesizes many of the insights of current work, while rejecting some of the excesses associated with particular interventions. The perspective that emerges is intended to support the idea that critical theory, in the tradition that runs from Marx to Habermas and Feenberg, still has something worth saying about technology. At the same time, it is perhaps the central argument of the book that this tradition needs to free itself from a deeply ingrained suspicion of technology, in particular of the attitudes and thought processes that make it possible. Contemporary scholarship in a number of areas, including feminist theory and political economy, makes it possible to leave behind romantic worries about technology as a branch of human endeavour and instead to situate it within the range of a normative critique of human social organization.

Technology is something that arises wherever there are human beings living together in societies. Power too has been present in all known human societies. Both are, like language, endemic features of the human condition. The earliest human societies were hunter gatherers, who lived a nomadic lifestyle based on taking what they needed from the environment, rather than applied processes of cultivation. Even in these non-hierarchical societies, there was technology in the form of axes, bows and arrows and cooking implements (Panter-Brick *et al.* 2001). Technology and power are implicated in one another historically and in contemporary social arrangements. There is no experience of technology that is not at the same time an experience of a kind of social power, but it does not always involve domination – the kind of power that concerns critical theorists. Moreover, there are instances of social and political power that have little or nothing to do with technology. I think that this proposition has not been well digested in the critical theoretical tradition, where "instrumental reason" has served as a convenient explanatory catch-all for the ills of capitalism and modernity. In this introduction, I will say more about the meaning of the terms "technology" and "power" as they are used in this book, before providing a brief overview of the chapters that follow.

Technology and Human Nature

We cannot imagine people living together who do not share a common physical infrastructure which they use to enhance their relations with the environment. Tool use is an anthropological given of the human species and it is something that we have in common with other, related species. Chimps, for example, have been observed sharpening sticks which they then use to spear fruit. They will even create a stock of such sticks prior to using them. This intentional fashioning of physical objects, aimed at using them subsequently to gain better leverage over other objects is an essential part of technology. Making and using tools are not all that there is to technology, however. In the definition just put forward, there is also the idea that the resulting stock of tools comes to define a society's way of relating to its environment. Tools become incorporated into a way of life, with its patterns and routines. In this way, they become technology. Technology is a culturally specific combination of the elementary anthropological disposition to create and use tools and the way of life of a social group.

This definition highlights the fact that technology is always both socially constructed and sociologically determinate. It can only be used and become a part of the fabric of life for human beings because it has been invested with significance for them. By taking on meaning in this way, technology enters human relationships and practices rather than appearing to be just inert matter or a kind of physical obtrusion. Toothbrushes, for example, are technological artefacts. They are part of dental hygiene for twenty-first century humans. As such, possession of a toothbrush signifies cleanliness and care for one's self, perhaps even a degree of independence. In consumer society, we choose toothbrushes with different styles and colours and the sense I have of this being "my" toothbrush involves feelings that go beyond issues of public health. In all these ways the toothbrush is a cultural construct – it means things to us as the people who use it. It could have meant other things. Small brushes with long handles can be used for other purposes, for example, but we call them toothbrushes and in so doing incorporate them into our practical existence in a specific way. At the same time, the toothbrush is not without consequences that derive from its own properties as an artefact. The first toothbrushes were made from pig bristles embedded in wooden handles and were made in China, probably in the sixteenth century (Curtis 1996). Prior to this and after it in different places around the world, people of different cultures seem to have used special kinds of wood or shell in conjunction with various tooth powders to keep their teeth clean. European adaptations of the Chinese idea, using softer bristles, begin from the late eighteenth century and in the 1930s nylon bristles and plastic handles began to be used. What is clear from this historical sketch is that changes in the design of the technology can have great consequences. Modern Europeans have much better teeth than their forebears, who do not seem to have brushed until relatively late compared to people elsewhere in the world. Combined with the emergence of scientific dentistry, the toothbrush is a member of a set of physical events that includes more healthy and durable teeth, as well as a social construct. Viewed as such, its properties are best-described in terms of dental science.

The example also highlights one point of connection between technology and social power. Toothbrushes enhance our leverage over events and processes in the world, enabling us to control the tendency for our teeth to decay if they are not cleaned regularly. As such they give us a basic kind of power over things, whereby we can bring about states of affairs that would not otherwise have been brought about, or forestall events that would otherwise have occurred. It is important to notice that this is a kind of social power and not a development of the human relationship with nature that can be understood independently of social mediation. A number of social factors are relevant in the toothbrush case. It is true that for centuries human beings had been scraping their teeth clean with some kind of recognized implement. As a deeply ingrained historical practice, this almost certainly has an evolutionary basis, with scraping emerging as the superior technique to, say, swilling out with some kind of fluid. However, alterations to teeth-cleaning practice had to be introduced and meet with approval from the population. These are social processes and they cannot be explained away with reference to the "obvious" benefits of brushing – there are too many examples of obviously beneficial techniques that lie neglected and of destructive techniques that became popular for us to accept such a line of explanation.[1] To understand the circumstances in which the modern toothbrush was shaped, we must examine the kinds of issue that would make such an artefact appealing in the context that human beings actually operated in at the time. Eighteenth century-Europe was the home of the coffee shop and the new sugar industry (Walvin 1992). People there had sugar-coated teeth and must have enjoyed the cleaning sensation of Addis's first brush in the 1780s. Moreover, the people who bought the brushes were the right people, namely, the fashionable new class of merchants who were in the process of creating a new social order (capitalism) that included a place for fashion and a new emphasis on making things that could sell. This social context is necessary to a full understanding of the toothbrush. The efficacy of the artefact – its capacity to effect specific kinds of change – is inseparable from its acceptance and incorporation into social practice. Given this, however, its consequences are also physical and work independently of that context. It is a central theme of this book that the way technologies mesh with social power always involves this kind of interplay of social construction on one side and the independent causal powers of artefacts on the other.

It is important to emphasize that these two aspects of technology reflect different approaches and methodologies, rather than substantive moments in the life of technological objects. Technological artefacts are always physical objects whose elements stand in causal relation to other physical entities. The technologist who understands how a machine or artefact works will approach it using descriptions that emphasize this. Technology users, on the other hand, will more commonly be concerned with what they have to do with the artefact in order to achieve their objective. This second approach involves being trained to view the object in a certain way, understanding its culturally constructed meaning and then incorporating it into routines and practices. To achieve this, we describe the technology in terms of its meaning for us as users. Light switches, for example, *either* lead into an account of circuitry, domestic wiring and the national grid *or* they become incorporated into the simple action of "turning on the light". The meanings we attach to the apparatus depend on us – who we are and how we approach the technology – and not the object. Statements about the technology have meanings relative to our purposes in the situation. The true statement that "the light is off" can mean that a diagnostic test has been run on a circuit or that we can begin our game of murder in the dark. The co-existence of these levels of description, each embedded in a different kind of social practice and responsive to different kinds of practical engagement with the world yet each reliant on the same set of truth-conditions reflects a deeper philosophical issue that also arises in connection with the issue of social power.

Social Power

Power is an endemic feature of human societies because some of its most profound manifestations reflect the fact that we are in a natural physical world that imposes limits on our freedom. Human beings are thinking rational agents who want to exercise free choice. In Immanuel Kant's terminology, we want to be autonomous (Kant 1993). However, as embodied creatures in a world of limits and pain, we must adjust to the causal order of the world. We are limited by mortality, illness and impediments set by the physical world. Technology is one response to this antinomical situation. Through it we can bring about changes in the physical world and make it a more amenable place, somewhere we can live more in accordance with our reason. This corresponds to the social and cultural level of description, which provides the motivation for technology development. However, achieving this goal involves creating a new physical environment that, while more accommodating, brings with it another causal context that involves new limits. This context is set out in the physical terminology of the technologist. Technology frees us from one set of physical constraints and sets us down in the midst of another. As such, it is involved in the mediation and reconfiguration of social power as a factor in history. A further implication of the distinction between levels of description put forward here is that some people in society may be in a better position to benefit from technology than others because they have a superior understanding of its inner workings. This becomes a particularly important issue in societies where science is a specialized activity. In these societies, there is a wide gap between understanding how a technology works and being a skilled user. This gap would not exist in societies where technically relevant knowledge was socially diffuse. In modern societies, however, it is a gap that widens and is populated with an array of possible subject positions – computer hackers and software users, for instance, have very different kinds of expertise in relation to the same artefact.

This highlights a further kind of power that arises in connection with technology, namely its use to enhance the position, status and wealth of some groups in society over others. In industrial societies, this was the result of a combination of social organization and technology design. Workers were brought together into factories and their energies combined in the operation of machines constructed on a larger scale than anything seen before, and drawing on new power sources, especially steam (Hobsbawm 1999; Misa 2004). Confronted with these machines, workers could only take the places assigned to them, rather than attempt to find a comfortable way of working or explore the machine for afford-ances and modes of operation not made explicit by the designer. Indeed, part of technology design is precisely the art of making clear to the user what they can and cannot do with it. Technology design always involves both a closing off of the technology's innards into a "black box" and the projection of messages on its outer surface that will guide the user into successful operation of the artefact. There is a concealed politics here, akin to statecraft. How technological artefacts are presented to users involves a politics of design that reflects features of the social context. It is here that we find the politics of the relationship between techno-logy and social power. As Andrew Feenberg (2002) argues, the politics of technology design calls for a model of analysis akin to the critical reading of political discourse. We should be as attentive to the design statements made through technology as we are to the actions of politicians.

Just as technology is a universal feature of human societies, the idea of a society without power is unthinkable. This is partly due to the inherent relationship between the two. As Fichman (1993) and others point out, the presence of technology always involves some kind of social organization. There can be no fishing nets, for example, without people prepared to get together, climb on board boats and brave the seas in pursuit of fish. This involves power, whether it is mediated by local market mechanisms, as in pre-modern rural fishing economies, or intensively supervised and managed by corporations who sell virtual fish on world markets, as happens in today's globalized economy. The employment of technology always involves social organization in which individuals are objectively required to assume specific roles and to engage in practices associated with those roles and this always involves power.

The liberal-pluralist conception of power, advanced originally by Robert Dahl, defines it as the capacity to act in such a way that other people then do things that they would not otherwise have done (Lukes 2005: 16). It is obvious that tools have been involved in the exercise of this kind of power. When power comes down to a show of force, posses-sion of the right tools can be decisive. This definition of power makes it semantically equivalent with control and coercion. Power is the ability to steer events in the direction that we want them to go. Tools are, in part, enhancements of the power of their users in connection with physical events. Tool use is closely related to, possibly a sub-set of, the actions that involve this kind of power. Military technology obviously constitutes a particular extension of this form of power. More advanced weaponry enables its possessor to compel those who do not have it to obey their orders. History affords us many examples of this use of superior tools to exercise what Lukes calls one-dimensional power.

The one-dimensional definition of power, however, reveals little about the actual extent to which technology as such is implicated in its operations. Dahl's definition was criticized by political theorists for neglecting a second dimension to the operation of power. This involves influence and authority, rather than force and coercion. Analysis of two-dimensional power draws attention to the way that compliance is secured from subject populations by making them perceive the world in such a way that certain questions are not asked. Exercise of this kind of power proceeds not by making threats but by suppressing problems before they are thematized in any public discourse. If two-dimensional power is used effectively, the result will be that people are influenced into doing what the powerful want them to do, or they may simply see it as the obvious right thing to do. Here it is not necessary to deploy a superior capacity for violence in order to exercise power. As Lukes puts it:

> *Influence* exists where *A*, "without resorting to either a tacit or an overt threat of severe deprivation, causes [*B*] to change his course of action". In a situation involving *authority*, "*B* complies because he recognises that [*A's*] command is reasonable in terms of his own values" – either because its content is legitimate and reasonable or because it has been arrived at through a legitimate and reasonable procedure.
>
> (2005: 21–22, quotes from Bachrach and Baratz 1970)

Understanding the workings of two-dimensional power involves attention to what is not said, to choices that are not made, to the pre-structuring of social choices so that some outcomes are made much more likely than others. Technology is extensively involved in the kind of ordering of the world in accordance with certain interests that is the exercise of two-dimensional power. Consequently, industrial machinery stimulates critical reactions from those who have to use it and from social critics. The tangible sense of indignation in Karl Marx's descriptions of nineteenth-century factory inspector reports frequently bears out the idea that technology is a mode of exercising social power and that this power can and sometimes should be resisted. The Luddites were not the only people to denounce technology as an agent of social power; their fame (or more commonly, notoriety) derives from the fact that in resisting that power they targeted the machines and tried to destroy them. Their struggle and those of other workers who found work with heavy industrial machinery was life-threatening in a physical or economic sense, is part of the definition of two-dimensional power. According to Lukes, the presence of some such symptomatic conflict signifies its presence in the situation.

What distinguishes three dimensional power from the two dimensional version is that there may be no symptom for power to be present. In other words, three dimensional power can be exercised without exciting public resistance, because people either do not notice it or are incapable, for whatever reason, of doing anything about it. Moreover, Lukes says, it can be significant from the perspective of critical social thought even in the absence of awareness of it and attempts at resistance. Indeed, it is part of the function of social criticism to attempt to make the machinations of power visible and to provide analyses that might enable people to initiate debates and mount challenges to the obvious and the taken for granted. This kind of thinking about power has a bearing on technology design and use. Technology has been subjected to exactly this kind of critique by some of the major thinkers of the twentieth and twenty-first centuries.

Most of the time, productive, work-related technology is not questioned by its users. They take it for granted as the prime determinant of their actions and conform to the rhythm imposed on them by the machines without discussing the matter in a way that would turn it into a political issue. However, this absence of thematization in public discourse conceals the exercise of power through machinery. The fact that this is not made into a matter for sustained debate reflects the way that three-dimensional power operates. Elaboration of this involves the notion of hegemony, developed by the twentieth-century Italian Marxist, Antonio Gramsci. Hegemony is secured through a strategic politics aimed at pre-structuring social practices in line with the interests of one's own group. This involves a "war of position" in which the power of description plays a central role. Different social classes compete to have their descriptions of a situation accepted as the most reliable. In this way, they try to normalize practices and routines, making them seem like the "right ones" for all members of society rather than just the way of doing things that best suits them. Normally in politics this does not involve trying to forge completely new kinds of rhetoric, or positioning oneself as having an entirely new way of looking the world. That would be off-putting to most people. The war of position involves trying to seize control of key concepts that are already widely used by people to make sense of life in their society. These concepts are, like power itself, essentially contested, while at the same time they reflect and embody interests that can be generalized onto society as a whole. In politics these ideas include the notions of reasonableness, social justice and fairness, and, in recent times, of an appropriate concern for the environment. No party wants to run an election campaign in which they openly deny any concern with these issues, or espouse a revolutionary distance from them in principle. Hegemony is secured by convincing the populace that the perspective taken on social justice by a particular class or party is the one that is most consistent with the interests of society as a whole. Once secured, hegemony takes the form of *consensual domination*, in which the ruling class enjoys power not because it has superior physical force but because it has successfully imposed its definitions or "articulations" (Laclau 1977) of the terms that all are agreed ought to apply. Andrew Feenberg (2002) has argued that this concept applies to technology design and this idea is a central theme of the current book.

Power in Lukes's discussion is always a normative concept. It is "ineradicably value-dependent" (2005: 30). Defined merely as the capacity to affect others, power is an anodyne concept, lacking sufficient purchase to single out significant instances as important. Part of the way that competing political viewpoints contest power and its application is by offering different criteria for significant manifestations of it in society. In this book, I will make use of Lukes's work, to explore the kinds of power that are exerted in the design of technological artefacts and the extent to which the exercise of social power more broadly construed can involve technologies, often as part of a strategic rendering of significant parts of the world unproblematic and beyond the scope of social critique and political opposition. I will suggest that the implication of technology design in strategies of power is real but that the two domains are not as dependent as we might be tempted to think. I do not want to forget the example of the humble toothbrush. The toothbrush is certainly a social and cultural product, with a history in which it takes on symbolic significance. The rise of the toothbrush is probably dependent upon the historical emergence of the bourgeoisie and of capitalism as a principle of social organization. Despite this, it is not obvious that toothbrushes are socially problematic. No one contests their utility and their design has not been politicized by any oppositional group. They enhance our ability to live in the world, since no one likes having toothache or bad breath, and as such their mass production and circulation are surely progressive in the sense that the toothbrush serves an interest that is shared by everyone. Hence, while the toothbrush does not stand outside social relations of power, any sensible critical assessment must concede its neutrality and that standards of efficiency in toothbrush design are probably best determined by dentists. The toothbrush turns out to be a kind of limit case for sociology of technology, since the salience of similar items effectively exonerates technology from the role assigned to it by much critical theory as a mono-causal source of evil in the social world.

The real test of relevance for technology critique is Lukes's test for the critique of domination. It involves stating the implied counterfactual to the situation under analysis. If we cannot show that the situation in question would be better for some or all of the relevant social actors in the absence of a given technology design, then we cannot mount a serious critique. Taking this pragmatic approach I hope, in what follows to contribute to a critical theory of technology that has a built-in standard of relevance, is not suspicious of technology because it is technology, and accepts the priority of scientific–technical explanations in our under-standing of the world. At the same time, the theory should be critical in the sense that it enables us to pinpoint occasions where technology design and its consequences are matters of serious concern and to clarify forms of agency relevant to challenging and questioning technology in contemporary society.

Overview of Chapters

The distinction drawn here between the technologist's level of descrip-tion and that of the user who is concerned more with the practical significance of technology is used in Chapter 2 to address some prob-lems in the philosophy of technology. Very often, we use technology without understanding it, how it works, where it came from or its place in the broader social system. This is why the philosopher Martin Heidegger famously said that we are "thrown" in technology, only noti-cing its inner workings when they malfunction and we fail in our intended actions as a consequence. If we want to understand what technology means to our culture we need to step back and compare it with the tools and artefacts of other historical cultures. The chapter contrasts Heidegger's view of technology as the destiny of modern societies with constructionist perspectives that emphasize the role of proximal, contin-gent factors which determine the significance of technical artefacts for their users on a case-by-case basis. Viewed in this way, technology is actively shaped by human beings, rather than the other way around. In the discussion I argue that the constructionist approach neglects the larger question of what technology is, as distinct from other classes of object and other areas of life. All technology is grounded in a certain disposition to the world, namely one that tries to establish affordances in the world by reconfiguring it some way. The purposes and inten-tions behind this activity, like its results, are contingent and variable and related to what each technology means in its cultural setting but the basic orientation to change the world in order to wrest something from it, is not.

Chapter 3 explores the claims that have been made for technology in making modern societies distinctive. Modernity involves unprecedented use of technology in three areas of social life: production, rational organization and communication. The chapter shows how these themes relate to significant technological developments in early modern Europe and how they inform different ideas of cultural modernity in classical, nineteenth-century sociology. The chapter concludes with a brief discussion of Jürgen Habermas's theory of social evolution and a comparison of his views with those of Feenberg, for whom Habermas's work constitutes a regression in critical theory's understanding of the relation between technology and modernity. Karl Marx was the first thinker to explicitly focus on technology and assign it a central explanatory role in relation to other social and cultural developments. In Chapter 4, I examine the work of critical historians and sociologists who have examined the role of technology in consolidating capitalist hegemony in modern industry. Work on production lines, for example, involves workers assuming subordinate positions in relation to the labour process as a whole, which has been structured prior to their arrival at the plant. Within this process machines are central. The labourer is subordinate to this design and, in consequence, enters the labour process as "an appendage to the machine". This is an instance of the exercise of two-dimensional power because it is a consequence of the social arrangements that surround the buying and selling of labour power in capitalist societies. Once you have signed up to be an industrial worker, you accept a situation that has been structured in advance. It makes no sense to become an industrial worker and then not comply with the demands of the machinery you are presented with – compliance is hegemonic. This chapter and the next also examine some feminist writing on technology. For these theorists the alignment of technology with prevalent norms of masculinity informs technology design. In this way, technology has concealed and reproduced male power in the workplace. At the same time, feminist scholarship has highlighted possibilities for the development of counter-strategies within technology design itself.

It is important to notice at this point that, in addition to being a vehicle or embodiment of social power, technology is also, in the examples given above, itself being shaped by power. Chapter 5 extends the discussion of social constructionism to take in feminist and "post-humanist" theorists. Prominent contemporary theorists have argued that digital technologies are uniquely open to being shaped by social power. This is both a danger and an opportunity, since it might herald an era in which humanity is subordinated to the logic of its own creations but it could equally be an opening to a new era in which personal autonomy is radically extended through technology as prosthesis. For the thinkers discussed in this chapter, the new situation poses a challenge to traditional categorical, or world-ordering distinctions. Organic/inorganic; subjective/objective; intelligent/inert; male/female – all are actively undermined in the development of technology with porous interfaces, in which even ideas like power and freedom seem to be being renegotiated by cyborg complexes that are neither human nor machine. As well as discussing Donna Haraway and N. Katherine Hayles's ideas, this chapter also discusses Bruno Latour's Actor-Network Theory in the context of this movement within recent social theory towards the idea of "post-humanity". This is the thesis that humans, machines and other objects should not be distinguished analytically by social scientists. From this perspective there is no reason in principle to think that humans are the only kind of entity that can engage in meaningful action, for example. This proposition is part of a broader argument according to which the social field has become flattened into a kind of surface on which we can see networks of association, but beneath which we can discern none of the tensions that once motivated critical thought. The chapter concludes with a critical assessment of these ideas that insists on the enduring character of technology and the human as discrete categories and denies that recent changes warrant the kind of drastic overhaul to our knowledge systems advocated by these authors.

The "post-human" thesis has been related by a number of thinkers to the idea that digital artefacts differ from traditional media objects in offering no foothold for rational critique. Chapter 6 examines the idea that digital aesthetics collapse the distance between technology and its users that is essential for the latter to critically appraise the former. It explores recent writing on the idea of a distinctive social aesthetics associated with digital culture and mainly promoted through the idea of "virtuality". Virtual objects engulf their users, allowing them to act on them and modify them from within, rather than subjecting them to critical scrutiny in the manner of a traditional reading. The chapter concludes, however, that the common video game is a more representative window on digital culture and that through analysis of its aesthetics we can identify resistance and critique reworked as moments in a process that is characteristic of technology use in the digital era. The final chapter relates this discussion of digital aesthetics to Feenberg's call for a new aesthetics of technology design and to developments within the economy associated with informationalism and globalization. Drawing on the work of Saskia Sassen, I argue that Feenberg's notion of progressive, or democratic rationalization is of the utmost significance to contemporary critical theory. Where other theorists seem intent on renouncing the goal of critique altogether while embracing a technical determinist appraisal of the digital as some kind of aesthetic panacea, Feenberg has identified a positive place for technical reason in opposition to capitalism. In Chapter 7, I argue that the challenge for technical politics is not to overcome technocracy, as formulated by Marcuse, but to address a more complex set of shifting horizons on technology development. In her analysis of the modern globalized economy, Sassen highlights the role of different cultures of interpretation in shaping digital technologies. These cultures are far from equal in terms of their possession of capital resources necessary to secure hegemony. However, the inventiveness and ingenuity of the resource-poor remains, as always, the main source of hope. Contemporary struggles demonstrate a new, redeemed role for technical reason which seems increasingly to be both the servant of capital and its most effective critic.

The Meaning of
Technology

The aim of this chapter is to use some ideas from philosophy to pin down what technology is and how technological artefacts come to be meaningful to human societies and individuals. Two views have been important to recent thinking. The first is substantivism, which identifies technology closely with modernity. For substantivists, modern societies are uniquely technological and to a large extent this determines the nature of life in those societies. What technology means, then, is the way of life specific to modern culture. This monolithic view contrasts with the approach of social constructionists, for whom the meaning of technology as a whole is an irrelevant, even metaphysical question. From a constructionist perspective the meaning attributed to or invested in specific technical artefacts is always thoroughly contingent on the intentions and practices of the human agents who work with it and use it and not projected by technology itself. However, constructionists lose sight of what connects all the different instances of technology, so that what particular technical artefacts signify to people is exhausted by the proximal meanings they take on in the course of being used. This means that we lose any overall, historical sense of what technology is and, importantly, what it ought to be.

A central theme of this chapter is that technical artefacts always feature in two ways of thinking about the world that are in tension with one another. We encounter technology as a source of imperatives as well as opportunities; like nature itself it requires us to do certain things and can constitute a limit on our freedom of manoeuvre. At the same time, technology is always something we incorporate into our intentional actions and meaningful projects. This means it is ambiguous between two modes of rationality. The first is causal and instrumental – we must understand how this part of the world works in order to use it properly. The second is meaning-oriented – we are doing something that matters to us and the context for this is the cultural context within which we are working. Technology is always both a reconfiguration of elements in the physical world and a part of social life for its users. As such, it can be described in the causal idioms of physical science and in terms of its use by social actors concerned with what it enables them to do rather than how it achieves this. The meaning of technology can be read off from how a society organizes the intersection of these aspects. This involves taking technology, or more precisely a technological orientation, as a kind of anthropological given, and incorporating it into our understanding of interpretation as the source of meaning in human affairs.

The section "Between Language and Instrumentalism" introduces pragmatist philosopher John Dewey's analogy between natural language and tool use. Dewey's perspective enables us to clarify the place of technology in society, positioning it somewhere between science and culture. The next two sections explore the substantivist definition of technology, drawing on the work of Heidegger and others who have identified it with meanings specific to and determinate for the modern cultural context. The second section "The Substantivist View" discusses Heidegger's idea that we are "thrown" in technology and that for modern people it defines our whole way of experiencing the world. The third section "Culture and Meaning" examines developments of this perspective in the work of Don Ihde and Albert Borgmann. These thinkers deepen Heidegger's approach, each drawing out different aspects of technological experience as central to life in cultural modernity. In the fourth section "Constructionism and the Meaning of Technology" the substantivist perspective is contrasted with constructionism, for which there is no single meaning of technology, but rather each artefact may be invested with many different meanings depending on the context. While this view has the pleasing effect of prioritizing human, meaning-making activities in the shaping of technology, it tends to lose sight of the features that define technology as a branch of human endeavour. In the fifth section "Hermeneutics of Technology", I suggest developing Dewey's analogy enables us to understand how technology fits into human social relations and take on the significance it does for its users. This turns out to be similar to Andrew Feenberg's thesis that technology is ambivalent between instrumental neutrality and implication in social organization, which is the topic of the final section "Dual Aspect Theory".

Between Language and Instrumentalism

Technology is a necessary feature of all human societies. Wherever there have been people living in communities with one another, there have

been modifications to the physical world resulting in material artefacts that are useful to members of the community and which, in their
design and structure, reflect the way of life of those people. A human
society without any kind of technology is as inconceivable as one without
language. Don Ihde writes that," ... human activity from immemorial
time and across the diversity of cultures has always been technologically embedded" (Ihde 1990: 20). While it takes its place in local cultures
of interpretation and use, technology is also an anthropological given
and constitutes a continuous strata within the historical process. We are
sometimes encouraged to think of some peoples as having no technology, or as having more "primitive" technology than others but it pays to
be suspicious of these ideas. There is little doubt that people everywhere
and throughout history have developed sophisticated technical apparatus
for a wide variety of purposes.

Like language, technology is an "all or nothing" feature of the human
condition. Language is an evolved trait of the human animal but is
fundamentally different from, say, the copying behaviour of parrots and
ravens. We do not acquire words and grammatical rules one after the
other, but all at once as the "language instinct" (Pinker 1994). Similarly,
there is a radical distinction to be drawn between technology, which is
a social practice, and simple tool use, which need not be. Technology
cannot be understood on the basis of a "building block" approach, with
sufficient density of tool use constituting a society as technological. The
relevant evolutionary step would have involved selective retention not
simply of a single routine practice, but of the impetus and mechanism
for intervention in the material physical world with the aim of expressing
and realizing complex projects. There is an evolutionary process to be
observed within these structures (language and technology) once they
have been established – languages too change and adapt – and this
takes us from stone axes to wind farms. But stone axes formed part of a
complex way of life with rules and meanings. The seeming simplicity of
the tool betrays nothing of the complex situation of which it was a part.
Hence, for example, in Iron Age Europe copper axe heads were signs
of high status, even though they were less effective cutting implements
than iron ones. This is a clue to the implication of technology in culture.
Tools are invested with significance and they transmit this significance
to their bearers and users. In this way they are caught up in a web of
meaning that is uniquely human. Technology is not just complex tool
use, it is, like mind and language, part of what defines us as humans.

Technology involves and is involved in public communication of a
kind that distinguishes human beings from other animals. This link to
language has been observed by thinkers who have tried to work out what
technology is and where it fits into our understanding of human society.

The pragmatist philosopher John Dewey famously described language as "the tool of tools", by which he meant that language allowed us to act upon the world in ways that are more complex than but not fundamentally different from using hammers and machines (Dewey 1997: 140). His proposition also entails the idea that human tool use is a subset of the skills that are involved in language use. That is to say that technology goes on within a context of public communication and makes sense because it conforms to rules that are specific to that context. This independence has limits, of course, because when we use technology we are obliged to work with materials that may be more or less resistant to our intentions. Even so the comparison holds since our own voice can sometimes fail us due to physical factors beyond our control and the sense of being thwarted that results is not radically different from finding that a programme will not run, or (I imagine) that wood is an insufficiently robust material to fabricate a helicopter. The common thread that links these situations is that coherent projects – singing, running a programme or flying – are developed and tried against a background of established practice and prior knowledge. Like writing or speaking, they only make sense against that background. Technology as a practice presupposes the presence of a cultural context, of which it is a fundamental and necessary part.

At the same time, regardless of cultural context, technology always seems to be about gaining leverage over the world in various ways. We use tools to enhance our control over nature and to achieve things we might otherwise not be able to achieve. Dewey gives a clear statement of this view:

> By its nature technology is concerned with things and acts in their instrumentalities, not in their immediacies . . . A tool is a particular thing, but it is more than a particular thing, since it is a thing in which a connection, a sequential bond of nature is embodied . . . Only through this bond does it sustain a relation to man himself and his activities. A tool denotes a perception and acknowledgement of sequential bonds in nature.
>
> (Dewey 1997: 103)

Technology is produced through action on a physical world that conforms to causal laws and it is produced by an animal that has certain interests and concerns. This is not to deny historical and cultural variation, but it is to assert that there is a kind of common basis on which we can understand better what that variation means and where it comes from. This is the understanding that some objects are to be understood, or interpreted in terms of their instrumentalities rather than their immediate appearances. It is not science, but it is clearly both a driver of scientific knowledge and a beneficiary of it. Scientific knowledge is descriptive and explanatory. It is produced in the context of social actions and practices that make it meaningful to scientists. When we take a scientific statement to be true and reliable, pragmatism tells us that this is because it is backed by a consensus among scientists (Peirce 1998: 115, 155). However, scientific knowledge does not act upon the world. That is the function of technology. Technology is a kind of system of statements made through objects and people acting in a certain way. What distinguishes the technological way of acting is that, unlike science, it is not constrained by the ideal of saying true things, but rather united around a common objective or purpose, which is making events occur that would not otherwise have occurred. The events need not be specified in advance; the point is that whereas science aims at truth, technology tries to create new events. Scientists try to speak the truth, technologists to effect change in the world.

The Substantivist View

The account just given naturalizes technology to the human animal and posits a fundamental continuity between instances of technology in history and across cultures. This continuity presupposes a human nature that involves intentional manipulation of the physical world to achieve desired ends. The philosopher and critic of modernity Martin Heidegger famously rejected attempts to define technology like this. For him, they represent superficial accounts that take appearance for reality and overlook the real significance of technology in modern societies. Heidegger distinguishes between the instrumentalist definition of technology, which grounds it in anthropology, and his own position, which brings out the true significance of the phenomenon in the modern world. His starting point is the phenomenological principle of the priority of experience. The only things that exist for us, as objects of possible experience, are not given from outside, so to speak, but actively revealed by us in and through our intercourse with the world. Different modes of interaction with the world are associated with different experiences.

Starting from this perspective, Heidegger takes issue with the idea that humans have always acted on the world to produce intended outcomes, that is, instrumentally. While other readers of Aristotle find his use of the word *techne* seems to denote something like this in the ancient world, Heidegger discerns a radical discontinuity between classical and modern ideas. If we could feel *techne* as the Greeks felt it, if we could live in their world, we would realize that something quite different was going on:

> ...what is decisive in *techne* does not at all lie in making and manipulating, nor in the use of means, but rather in...revealing...It is as revealing and not as manufacturing that *techne* is a bringing-forth.
>
> (Heidegger 2004: 255)

In pre-modern times, Heidegger is saying, technical action gave rise to a distinctive experience of the world. This mode of experience was not the impoverished perspective of modern instrumentalism, although clearly it involved some of the things mentioned above like identifying affordances in the world, understanding them and working with them to achieve effects. The ancient experience of *techne* was compatible with a fundamentally different attitude towards being in general, it did not menace other ways of understanding by insisting on purposiveness. Modern technology seems to be intent on depriving non-technical ways of apprehending the world of their legitimacy by judging them in terms of their efficacy in achieving goals. *Techne*, Heidegger argues, was experienced as one way of revealing the world and as such was quite consistent with other kinds of revealing (Feenberg 2005).

The Heideggerian critique of the instrumentalist–anthropological view is that it is based on a facile extrapolation from the experience of tool use. Everyone knows what it is to use an object to bring about changes in their physical environment. Here the technology user is cast in the active role, while technology is viewed simply as inert or governed by the intentions of the user. This priority of the human is what Heidegger derides as the "anthropological" element in the definition. The point of his substantive critique is that technology is not something we encounter and use in this way. Technology is always an integral element of the world even before we act on it. Technological artefacts form part of the texture of our experience throughout our formative years. They are part of the stable fabric of the world we share with others. This world is one that we create in and through our activity – it is an experiential world – but we do not come at it afresh each time and reconstruct it from scratch. For Heidegger, this is an instrumentalist delusion. In fact, technology is naturalized for us, it meshes seamlessly with the rest of the physical environment and only becomes visible when it breaks down.

> The merely instrumental, merely anthropological definition of technology is, therefore, in principle untenable. And it may not be rounded out by being referred back to some metaphysical or religious explanation that undergirds it.
>
> (2004: 258)

We take it for granted that rooms have light switches and only reflect on the electrical system as technology, or in its instrumentality, when the light fails to come on because the bulb has broken or a fuse has gone. Normally, throwing the light switch simply *is* turning on the light. From our perspective as intentional agents, throwing the switch does not *mean* creating a connection and facilitating the flow of current to the filament in the bulb. Still less do we contemplate the values of the current or the conditions that have to obtain inside the bulb. This is why Heidegger says that we are always "thrown" in our technology. We live inside it, rather than coming at it from outside to manipulate the world in ways of our own choosing. The point of his comment about metaphysics and religion is that we cannot pretend that the instrumentalist account is true even though it does not comport with our experience. The fact that no one detaches themselves from the world in order to come back at it equipped with knowledge of electronic circuitry and intent on activating this knowledge to secure illumination is decisive. The act of throwing the light switch does not have this structure. Understanding it requires that we understand the culture within which this kind of activity is normal and obvious.

On this account, there is a clear discrepancy between the place that technology has in our lives – what it means to us – and the merely instrumental definition of what technology is. For Heidegger, this is a kind of clue to the real, *substantive* character of technology. As subjects of modernity, we think about it in the wrong way because our extensive reliance on technology as the only way to experience the world predisposes us to neglect the role of revealing. Technology use "...banishes man into the kind of revealing that is an ordering. Where this ordering holds sway, it drives out every other possibility of revealing" (Heidegger 2004: 261). As members of a society in which extensive technology use has made access to goods, like illumination, simple and convenient, we have lost our appreciation of the centrality of revelatory experience and of our own activity in determining that experience. We have closed off possibilities of revealing the world other than those that conform to the model of throwing a switch to get what we want. Modern culture is uniquely embedded in technology and in consequence we have a limited view of the world, which Heidegger calls "enframing". What is regrettable about technology is that it obscures or even destroys other ways of finding meaning. And the kind of life that it opens onto is one in which means and ends are separated so that we find ourselves performing instrumental routines aimed at consumption, rather than appreciating the full range of meaning possibilities available to us as a matter of existential fact. This is why technology is, for Heideggerians, a fateful destiny that is inconsistent with a more meaningful way of life. According to this view, we are always "thrown" in a technological culture and there is something wrong with the direction in which we are being propelled by technology. At the centre of this picture is the notion of experience. Technology use is all-encompassing and determinate so that it leads us into an enframed and therefore diminished "world". The sense of this is clarified by more recent work on the phenomenology of technology, in which the substantivist position is developed into a theory of the cultural meaning of technology.

Culture and Meaning

In a series of books Don Ihde (1990, 1991, 1993) has built on Heidegger's work, emphasizing the relativity of technology to what he calls its "praxical context". By this phrase he means to bring out the fact that technology only exists for us as a component part of experience and that what we are able to experience is contingent on the kinds of active involvement we have with the world. Part of that active involvement, of course, turns on the nature of our technology. In other words, we are always already "thrown" in a technological culture but we are also participants in the reproduction of that culture as a context. Hence, while he acknowledges that technology "must have some concrete component, some material element" (1990: 47), he stresses that,

> There is no thing-in-itself. There are only things in contexts and contexts are multiple . . .
> A technological object, whatever else it is, *becomes* what it "is" through its uses. This is not to say that the *technical* properties of objects are irrelevant . . .
> (Ihde 1990: 69–70)

According to Ihde, the interpretation of a technology is a matter of hermeneutics[1] – we have to find out what the technology means to its users if we are to understand it. In Heideggerian terms, we are trying to find what is revealed through a given technology and this requires a phenomenological investigation – one that focuses on the experience of technology use. The idea here is that by exploring the experience of "thrown-ness" we can discern what kind of a "world" technology is for us and what possibilities it excludes.

Ihde argues that we make technology disappear, or become transparent, when we incorporate it into our everyday action routines. He calls this process "embodiment" because when technology is transparent it feels like an extension of one's body. This transparency, however, is never complete because there are always glitches and breakdowns at some point in the embodiment relation. At this point, the technology will reappear in its objectness. An example of this might be riding a bicycle. Most of the time when we cycle we do not think about the processes of balancing, pedalling and steering. We are able to concentrate on where we are going or riding safely because those actions that involve the mechanical operation of the bicycle are within the scope of a simple intention, namely, to cycle. The bicycle has disappeared under that intention, and it has become transparent. However, when the chain comes off the bike, or we have a puncture, then we are forced to confront the machine as a piece of technology. In that moment of incomprehension that precipitates the perspective switch – when we realize we are not getting anywhere, or the bike is wobbling – the brute physicality of the bicycle as a machine obtrudes. Ihde argues that this is a feature of all technology use: "There is a ratio between the objectness of the technology and its transparency in use" (1990: 108). When objectness is dominant, "what remains is an obtruding, and thus negatively defined, object" (1990: 94).

When we fall out of the embodiment relation in this way, we find ourselves needing to reconstruct our relationship with the artefact we are using, on the basis of an alternative, explicitly technical approach. This requires a different attitude, in which we are alienated from the technology and have to draw on prior knowledge and experience to reposition the now problematic object within our perception of the world. It now appears as a thing, but one that is invested with meanings. It is important, for Ihde, to notice that these meanings are not abstract, but a function of our practical activity. For example, lenses and spectacles signify enhancements to the sense of vision and medical intervention to correct impairments to that sense. At the same time they constitute an enhancement of the visual sense that reflects a cultural bias towards the visual. As Ihde puts it, "new instrumentation gives rise to new perceptions" (1990: 56). Coming to terms with a bicycle breakdown involves being able to interpret the bicycle as an artefact and this presupposes a concern with mobility that I acquired from a culture that has many technologies of movement and transportation. Having got past the shock of experiencing the technology in its brute objectness, then, we come back at it with the aim of restoring it to its transparent condition of being taken for granted and comfortable. This involves viewing the bicycle as part of the world beyond myself. Then it appears as a problem to be solved and this can only be done if we know what the artefact is for, which is a function of the cultural context.

A similar approach to Ihde's has been advanced by Albert Borgmann, who argues (1984, 1999) that the modern experience of technology is based on our use of devices. Borgmann shares Ihde's belief in the usefulness of a phenomenological analysis of the experience of technology use as the method for establishing its significance. Technology cannot be analyzed independently of its effects on the human user; what it is, it is *for* someone and the character of that experience cannot be understood independently of them and their cultural context. For Borgmann, what characterizes our relationship with modern technology is its device character. He defines the device as follows:

> In a device the relatedness of the world is replaced by a machinery, but the machinery is concealed and the commodities which are made available by a device are enjoyed without the encumbrance of or the engagement with a context.
>
> (Borgmann 1984: 47)

The device paradigm bears obvious similarities to Ihde's notion that technology becomes transparent, or disappears in use. According to Borgmann, this is not brought about by embodiment, although nothing he says rules that out in connection with technologies specifically designed to merge with the body like false teeth or artificial limbs. These cases are not paradigmatic for Borgmann, but devices are. This is because, like modern capitalism itself they present their users with accessible commodities. The commodious character of technology is its ability to render services to us without our having to think about how this has been done. We press a button on the dashboard and the car's engine starts. We take control of the car and are able to travel without ever leaving the comfortable environment within. This may be air-conditioned for our comfort and it will almost certainly contain music and refreshments. Travelling is purged of its unpleasant aspects. In place of physical exertion in the face of unpleasant weather and other hazards, we are given a pleasurable experience. The work of the journey is done for us by the tyres, engine and so on.

Borgmann takes this function of relieving its user of onerous tasks to be definitive of technology. He uses the example of a music system:

> It is the division between the commodity, eg. music, and the machinery, eg. the mechanical and electronic apparatus of a stereo, that is the distinctive feature of a technological device.
>
> (Borgmann 1984: 4)

The commodious character of technology, he argues, is an inherent property that unfolds in the development of the modern world. Technology tends to conceal its mechanism, to reduce its scale in order to become less obtrusive. Technology projects itself as a commodity to be used and, in so doing it both "guides and veils" (1984: 39) the development of modern societies. It guides them in the sense that it is consistent with a culture based on consumption and it encourages the reproduction of that culture. It veils by concealing itself, its own inner workings, from view and in this way technology contributes to the development of a cultural context within which consumption and use are the dominant values. This seems strange because historically technology has not been aimed at consumers but centrally concerned with production. Surely, when a factory worker engages with a machine the relationship is not configured in the same way? Borgmann denies that there is a difference and insists that,

> Labour does not in general lift the veil of unfamiliarity from the machinery of devices. The labour process is itself transformed according to the paradigm of the device.
>
> (Borgmann 1984: 48)

The device may seem to oppress the worker by imposing its rhythm and routine of work onto them but it does not in the process enlighten them as to its underlying mechanisms. Even if it was true that having a workforce who understood how their machines worked was more efficient, the device paradigm would, on this account, militate against this.

For both these thinkers, as for Heidegger, what is significant about modern technology is not so much what it reveals as what it conceals. Both regret the passing of a more innocent time when technology did not have us in its grip, when experience of the world was unmediated by technical systems or devices. Hence, Borgmann argues that, "What distresses one about technology is its tendency to destroy or displace things and practices that grace and orient our lives" (Borgmann 1984: 157). To pursue the analogy with language suggested above, substantivists criticize modern technology for limiting the kinds of things we can say so that we can only conceive of the world in terms that make it usable or consumable. As Heideggerians, both Borgmann and Ihde maintain the possibility of a subjective position that is not mediated by life in a society that always already has technology. Only from such a perspective, it seems, might we be able to judge what technology conceals, even while it reveals new possibilities for leverage and control. However, I have suggested above that technology is an endemic feature of human societies and of the human condition. It is not clear that one can step outside of being technological and make claims about what its costs might be. Ihde's position on this is paradoxical, since he clearly states the impossibility of a life that is not "embedded" in technology and yet at the same time invokes the idea of a mythical character, named Adam, who represents humanity from the time before technology. According to Ihde, it is "possible for us to see both nakedly *and* mediately – and thus to be able to locate the difference", because, "we retain ... the ordering spatiality of Adam" (Ihde 1990: 79–80). In other words, although we have been powerfully shaped by technology and are normally thrown in a world that is characterized by the presence of technological systems and structures, when breakdowns occur we are able to step back from this and size up the world from a "natural" perspective. This echoes an idea from Heidegger, namely the quasi-religious principle of an unmediated confrontation with being shorn of all social and historical constructions (Adorno 1986; Dews 1987). The problem is that such a standpoint is an historical fiction; moreover it is one that makes something of a mockery of Heidegger's rejection of the idea of a metaphysical "undergirding" of the instrumental definition of technology. There is no stepping outside of history to a standpoint from which we can see how things would be without technology. The idea that there might be such a perspective, or that it would be useful is itself metaphysical and probably religious in its inspiration. It is much more useful to think about interpreting technology as part of a process of cross-cultural comparison and understanding, on analogy with linguistic translation.

Constructionism and the Meaning of Technology

Ihde's emphasis on the "praxical context" of technology positions his argument somewhere between substantivism and constructionism. If the substantivist view defines technology as something in which modern culture is "embedded" and through which modern subjects are "thrown" in an "enframed" perspective on the world, constructionists maintain that the reverse is true. Technology is actually embedded in culture, actively shaped by social actors who invest it with meanings and bend it to reflect the desires and interests of (non-technological) forms of collective life. Constructionism does not merely assert that discoveries, categories, artefacts or institutions have a social history. It attaches a particularly strong significance to the role of language in making those facts what they are. The decisive factor in the construction of facts and artefacts is their representation by social agents in language. How something is described turns out to be fateful for the ways in which people think about it; the expectations they have of it; the uses to which they will put it, and the projects they develop in response to its presence. This emphasis on language and representation, or labelling, is what defines social constructionism. The point is well expressed by Ian Hacking:

> Constructionists tend to maintain that classifications are not determined by how the world is, but are convenient ways in which to represent it. They maintain that the world does not come conveniently wrapped up in facts. Facts are the consequences of ways in which we represent the world.
>
> (1999: 33)

Applied to technology, the constructionist position involves identifying the social factors involved in the creation and use of a given technology. But more than this, it focuses on how the language people use to understand what they are doing in connection with the artefact plays an explanatory role in its development, determining what role it plays in human affairs.

According to Wiebe Bijker (1997), writing the social history of an artefact in constructionist terms involves identifying a series of steps or phases in its development. First, it will be possible to identify one or more relevant social groups who participate in defining the artefact, constituting it as a meaningful object and picking out certain of its possibilities. These groups will then be found to differ over its correct interpretation. Prototypes will be made and circulated, various possibilities will be discussed and there will be a dispute over such issues as what the thing could and should be used for, who should be allowed to use it and what design best meets these needs. During this phase the artefact is said to have "interpretative flexibility" (Bijker *et al.* 1989); its meaning-significance is open to be negotiated and contested by relevant social groups. Eventually, this period comes to a conclusion, normally with one interpretation of the artefact securing domination over the others. This interpretation fixes ideas of what the artefact is for and how it should be used and it determines subsequent designs of the artefact.

The history of the bicycle is often used to illustrate these ideas. The first bicycle seems to have been something of a baroque absurdity made by a French aristocrat in the late eighteen century (Bijker 1997: 21). It had no propulsion or steering mechanisms and had to be picked up and moved by its rider between convenient slopes and straight paths. This machine seems to have been made of wood and to have had evenly sized wheels. The first attempt to produce bicycles commercially came almost a century later. Famously, nineteenth-century bicycles were very bumpy and uncomfortable to ride because they had no proper tyres. One solution was to enlarge the front wheel, which gave added speed as well as absorbing some of the bumps. It was at this stage that the meaning of the bicycle was contested. Young men wanted faster bicycles and are said to have viewed the larger front wheels as signs of virility – they made riding the bike faster and more dangerous. Older men and female riders wanted something more practical and, literally, down to earth. The antagonism between these, the relevant social groups, was resolved during the forty years between the boneshaker and the "ordinary" safety cycle. Some role was played in this by the invention of the pneumatic tyre in 1888 by John Boyd Dunlop (Bijker 1997: 79). After this innovation bicycles with smaller front wheels were actually faster than the Penny Farthings and other large front-wheeled contraptions and so the interests of racing youth were reconciled with those of other cyclists in a series of new designs in which the wheels were of equal size. In this way the design of the bicycle secured "rhetorical closure"; it became fixed as the object with which we are all now familiar. Deviations and experiments in bicycle design have moved within these parameters for over a century now and we can confidently assert that this is what a bicycle is and what it should look like. A range of interests expressed as purposes are sedimented in the design, so that everyone knows a bicycle is a mode of transport suitable for getting around town and exercising. The racing use still persists as a specialist pursuit but the fundamentals of machine design are the same across all these cases.

Constructionism places great emphasis on the meanings of specific artefacts. To get from this to an understanding of what technology as a whole signifies, Bijker has attempted to situate the ideas of socially relevant group, interpretative flexibility and rhetorical closure, within a broader explanatory and critical framework. To achieve this, he invokes the concept of a "technological frame". The technological frame is the perspective taken on an object in its early stages of development by potentially diverse relevant social groups. From it they derive a common understanding of what the object is and of its possibilities. As an artefact is discussed and passes through the period of interpretative flexibility, it is the technological frame that makes discussion possible and ensures people are not simply talking past one another. The technological frame is a discursive system of reference or conceptual scheme which ensures that, while different social actors may want different things from the new technology they are nonetheless working together in the construction of a single, common object. As Bijker writes:

> A technological frame structures the interactions among the actors of a relevant social group. Thus it is not an individual's characteristic, nor a

characteristic of systems or institutions; technological frames are located between actors, not in actors or above actors. A technological frame is built up when interaction "around" an artefact begins.

(1997: 123)

This definition suggests that the sense people have of a thing being technology or technological is an emergent feature of specific social situations. In other words, people are not thrown in technology but actively involved in making it anew as they invest each new artefact with meaning and significance of their choosing.

The mobile phone is a useful example that can illustrate strengths of both substantivist and constructionist points of view. Mobile phones are on the face of it perfect examples of Borgmann's device paradigm. As Myerson (2001) points out, in the course of a decade (the 1990s) they became social necessities especially for young people in rich countries. The mobile was a desirable commodity whose mechanism was concealed behind a veneer of advertising that talked up their novelty and projected them as emblems of technological progress. The young people who acquired them were thrown in a new way of relating to one another, which often excluded older people, including family members. They entered a new technologically mediated way of relating to their friends and in this sense the technology enframed their view of society, with "network" metaphors becoming increasingly salient. However, from a constructionist perspective we can also see that mobiles took on significance for users that derive from their own, praxical engagements with it. While we can argue that the lives of mobile users are increasingly embedded in technology, it is equally viable to see them as shaping mobile phones by incorporating them into prior, meaning-giving structures. Hence, the mobile means different things to people in different cultural settings and there are even different rituals surrounding them in various parts of the world. Finnish teenagers, for example, are known to keep handwritten "diaries" of their text messages, something that does not seem to occur anywhere else (Kasesniemi and Rautiainen 2002). They were prompted to do this by the fact that mobiles have limited memories and the significance of some messages made it unpleasant to delete them. The technology was initially projected as a device but has become, through such assimilation processes, something quite different and unpredictable. Indeed, far from impoverishing the meaning of specific communicative acts, the mobile has here had the opposite effect. Things said in the early stages of a relationship, for example, would have simply been forgotten and lost if these teenagers had not been confronted with the physical possibility of losing them from their phones. This moment of alienation from the device promotes reflection and a culturally mediated response that incorporates it and changes its meaning. Texts sent to these mobiles may well gain a place in a handwritten memento – the very antithesis of Borgmann's enframing scenario.

The constructionist view, however, raises a bootstrapping issue, since it does not stipulate what would incline people towards recognizing their activity as technological or an object as technology in the first place. The decision that some activity or artefact is technological is determined by the group, without reference to any external, objective historical factors that connect up all the instances of technological practice. Bijker argues that technological frames serve as a kind of "hinge" between this, the "social interactionist perspective" of technologists, and society at large. In what he calls its "semiotic perspective", Bijker suggests that the frame also enables non-relevant social groups to find meaning in new and developing artefacts. The frame accommodates the constructed meaning of the technology and its significance for society at large. This explains how technology seems to be both permanent and durable, as material infrastructure so to speak, and a contingent social construction:

> By rendering the two sides of the analysis – social groups and technical artefacts – into aspects of one world, "technological frame" will be helpful in transcending the distinction between hitherto irreconcilable opposites: the social shaping of technology and technical determinism, society and technology.
>
> (1997: 197)

As artefacts are created by technologists and recognized by broader publics, so they come to assume their status as technology and the practices around them are understood as technical. The constructionist view defines technology as a social practice that involves objects and is defined as such through this bivalent system of social recognition. According to Bijker, even the criteria for whether an artefact works or not are emergent properties of the social situation in this way, since, "...the technological frame comprises the actor's criteria for 'working' and 'non-working' rather than our own hindsight knowledge" (1997: 124). While constructionism succeeds in detaching the significance of technology from any overarching destiny peculiar to modern societies, it actually goes too far in that it cannot account for the fact that the question "does it work?" always arises specifically in connection with technology.

The constructionist view also exaggerates the extent to which technology's appearance of solidity and incorrigibility is a social construct. Once constructed, a technical artefact will conform to physical laws corresponding to its materials and design. This is best understood by scientists and technicians, who approach artefacts with a focus on their formal properties, paying particular attention to the kinds of causal connection that can be found working within them and measurable features of their behaviour. This kind of interpretation brings out the correct way to use objects that have been intentionally configured by other human beings. This is why Bijker says that the semiotics of artefacts in use "mirror technological development" (1997: 197). Once stabilized and used in society, technologies come enveloped in a semiotic system that affirms the idea of technology as an unfolding, autonomous system. However, the constructionist view casts this as a consequence of the operations of social power, produced entirely by social processes.[2] Such a position actually obscures what is distinctive about the technological attitude to the world, regardless of historical setting.

Hermeneutics of Technology

Bijker's notion of technological frame is offered as a theory of the hermeneutics of technology, an account of how we recognize some things as technological and learn to relate to them as such. We know that something is technology when it comports with our culture's notion of what that is. This cues us to interpret it, or to approach it in a way that enables us to learn its practical significance. However, while it may be true that we learn how to distinguish technological affordances from those of nature, it seems counter-intuitive, even implausible to maintain that the distinction is merely conventional. Moreover, if the meaning of technology is contingent on the role it plays in our culture and our culture is embedded in technology then it will always be valid to approach everything as if it were technology, or never. Between these views there is the idea that humans everywhere interpret technology. Interpreting technology requires us to break into the web of meanings that surround it in its cultural setting.

The problem is similar to that faced by philosophers who are concerned with how meaning works in natural languages. There, what we see is a formal, material system (language) that somehow takes on meaning for its human users. The difficulty in both cases is to see how this happens – where does the meaning come from? The substantivist view is that technology enframes modern culture and orients its meaning-making capacities towards the merely instrumental: The meaning of technology in modernity is an attack on meaning. This notion of enframing has an analogy in philosophy of language in the idea that different languages carve the world up in different ways and are thereby determinate for the cultures in which they are spoken. Hence, Benjamin Lee Whorf argued that limitations of some workers' vocabularies made them more prone to industrial accidents, or that the languages of indigenous peoples were incommensurate with the organization of the world into discrete classes of object and event (Pinker 1994: 59). Languages are objective structures that incline us to view the world in culturally specific ways. However, as Donald Davidson (1984) and other philosophers have shown, a defining feature of natural language is precisely that there are no such incommensurabilities between them – part of what makes a language a natural human language is that what can be said in it may be expressed in any other such language. Something similar may be true of technology. People in different circumstances and with different theories about the world strive to achieve various ends, but they are all capable of understanding one another and of recognizing their interventions as having a common purposiveness. It is on this basis that we can understand what and how technologies "mean" to people.

In the philosophy of language, the "hermeneutic circle" is commonly addressed by taking the case of speakers of two radically alien languages as paradigmatic for all situations where meanings are exchanged. This case can only be addressed by bringing to bear certain assumptions about the underlying character of the situations we are observing. Analytical philosophers argue that the problem of "radical interpretation" is best addressed through application of the "principle of charity". This principle involves no attribution of substantive beliefs but urges that each must consider the other rational, in the minimal sense that they do not believe contradictories true,[3] and that they each assume that the other's beliefs are true by their own lights. The first of these principles is sometimes called "folk psychology". Underscoring the second is the belief that, since humans are hooked up to the material world in broadly identical ways and the physical world is a constant that obeys the same laws everywhere, so there will be a substantial body of truths on which members of all cultures and speakers of all natural languages will agree. This convergence constitutes a point of departure, from which meaning-interpretation is possible.

When we encounter a new technology, we have to be taught what it is for. Despite the good design practice of making the electrics inaccessible to users, most people have reflected at least once or twice on what actually goes on when we throw a light switch, perhaps especially during power cuts. Reflecting on the underlying structure of a technology in this way is normal and, in my view, is part of what defines technology for human beings. This means that we ask it some questions rather than others, try to achieve something with it rather than merely looking at it or playing with it. Just as with language, we cannot attribute any meaning to the structure of the technology device, or derive any significance from analyzing the causal relationships that make up its inner structure, but when the thing is made to work in context then we can use our understanding of the structure to guide us in interpreting the meaning it takes on for its users. At the same time, if we want to make sense of an artefact we need to ask what it is to be used for. If technology is like language, then assuming that there is a correct use for any given artefact is analogous to assuming that most of what people say is true and then finding that this enables us to see what they mean. Just as chasing "truth" is folly (cf. Davidson 2005a), except as a function of a language use in context, so chasing correct use in an ultimate sense is silly – there is no correct use for any artefact independent of its cultural setting. But part of interpreting a new technological artefact, be it alien because it comes from a strange culture, or just new to us, will always be asking ourselves, what should I do with this? How can I get the best use out of it? How do its users use it? When this attitude works, enabling us to achieve recognizable ends with the new device, then we are confirmed in our belief that it was technological. Learning to use the thing properly in this way, we will find out what it "means". Aimless exploration or just enjoying the feel of a new object will lead to certain kinds of experience with it, but they will not enable us to use it properly. It is a feature of art that it plays with our in-built desire to comprehend and find order in objects and the fact that we can move through a repertoire of approaches to achieve this – a theme I resume in Chapter 6. When we are sure that we can use an object it enables us to experiment further and to build up a map of its workings, or just to use it. Commonly, we do a bit of both.

Using technology properly is meaningful since it corresponds to taking one's place in a culture. At the same time, effective use of a technology is also technical. It entails acting on the physical world in a way that is causally efficacious. To interpret technology we must understand what changes it effects when it is used properly and what these changes and the ability to make them signify to the community that use that technology. One way of understanding these two aspects of technology would be in terms of a supervenience relation. Fundamentally, technology is described in terms of its physical properties and its capacities are explained in terms of the scientific principles of cause and effect. This is technology as described by physical science. The same processes can be described from the perspective of a concern with meaning, and in the terminology of contemporary analytical philosophy this description will supervene on the first. Meaning-oriented levels of description always supervene on physical ones because it is always possible in principle that a purely physical explanation could be produced for any set of events in the world, including the use of technology.[4] This means that physical descriptions have a kind of priority, since they provide true descriptions of the world. However, other modes of description and action are warranted by pragmatic features of the human situation (Evnine 1991). Social theory and social description respond to the practical human need we have to understand ourselves in a larger social context. As a discourse it invokes entities and classes of event (meaning, mind, thoughts, reasons) that are anomalous from a purely physicalist perspective, but which command assent as explanatory devices. The role of interpretation is to introduce meaning into situations that were simply present beforehand – as one of the founders of modern pragmatism, C.S. Peirce says, meanings are always located in "future time" (1998: 274). Similarly, G.H. Mead, the pragmatist philosopher and psychologist describes mind as a "functional hypothesis", rather than a fundamental category of being (1967: 10; See also McGinn 1982). Saying that meaningful interpretations supervene on other levels of description means that we acknowledge their character as useful, limit ourselves to those we can plausibly maintain are physical events under a different kind of description and do not ascribe to them a status as entities that exist over and beyond their physical occurrences. Substantivists, as we have seen, pay no attention to this last injunction and take the notion of discrete "worlds of meaning" around technology as a given, independent of what we know about the physical universe. Constructionists on the other hand, seem to deny that there is a physical universe beyond our linguistic constructions of it,[5] or at least that this physical world plays any role in constraining what we may, meaningfully say about it.

The strength of Dewey's definition (above) is that it enables us to extrapolate from the fact that all peoples use technology to certain core assumptions about human beings that disclose its defining features. According to this definition, technologies stand between the understanding or knowledge a community has of the world – its sequences or regularities – and their practical requirements. When we approach artefacts we know that they have been shaped by some guiding intention and that their users are trying to achieve something in the world. The artefact has an instrumental purpose designed into it and that this purpose reflects both the understanding a community has of the physical world and its attempts to realize certain purposes. These propositions hold for any technology whatsoever and when trying to make sense of technology they constitute a necessary, if mostly just assumed and unstated, starting point. If we did not assume them we would never be able to recognize that the operator of a machine was operating a machine, rather than just engaged in some bizarre choreography, still less to learn from them how to work the machine for ourselves. These assumptions have a kind of heuristic utility; we can use them to make out the practical meaning of any technology. The latter will of course be culturally variable, but the assumptions, which I call folk technology, are not. They enable us to identify the presence of technology in the first place. Folk technology defines technology in terms of an attitude taken by human actors towards things and states of affairs. This is not to deny historical and cultural variation, but it is to assert that there is a common basis on which we can understand better what that variation means and where it comes from.[6] In a sense, the meaning of our technology, or of technology in our culture, could only come into relief when we see another technology in another cultural setting. Just as with linguistic meaning, the meaning of a technology is a function of this operation of interpreting between technologies. At the same time, interpretation will work on the basis that the two systems share fundamental properties.

The calendar is a useful example that highlights the combination of relatively stable, continuous practical purposes and changing scientific knowledge in the design and construction of useful artefacts whose details vary between cultures.[7] According to Boorstin (1985), nearly all human societies have developed calendars, although the knowledge they have deployed and the cultural concerns embedded in their design have, of course, varied. The calendar is an artefact that develops and evolves in the intersection of practical and cultural requirements with human knowledge about the natural universe. Most calendar systems since the Babylonians have been based on understanding of astronomy especially the movements of the planets in relation to the sun (Bernal 1987). In an interesting cultural contrast, the Muslim calendar relies on measurements of lunar behaviour. Notwithstanding this cultural variation, it is still recognizably the same kind of artefact as the Christian calendar, relaying information about cycles of cosmological time in terms that have practical significance in a human cultural context, with its cycles and rhythms. At the same time, calendars have taken diverse forms, and these differences have assumed social and political significance. The French and Russian revolutions gave rise to attempts to alter calendars, to create the sense of a fresh start that encompasses the whole of society. These events show that calendars can be seen as enframing a culture or a way of life, in Heidegger's sense.

However, there is no revolutionary project dedicated to their elimination. To see what is wrong with a given calendar we do not step outside of calendarness altogether and look at the passage of cosmological and cultural time in a way that renounces the goal of measurement or refuses to recognize their cyclical character. Critical perspectives involve assuming the quasi-natural function of the calendar and of calendrical measurement as such and then comparing *this* calendar with some rival alternative, which might be based on a new set of terms or a new theory about the behaviour of astronomical bodies, or an alternative set of practical priorities. When the calendar in sixteenth-century Christian Europe began to slip out of step with the agricultural seasons it was deemed necessary to reform it (Boorstin 1985: 9).[8] The point is that there is no standpoint outside of this kind of device from which we would want to "start again", there is only an endless historical interplay of such devices mediated through positions that reflect changing concerns. The latter presuppose certain core properties of human beings, including the idea that we measure time to secure greater leverage over future events and in order to be able to talk coherently about past ones.

Dual Aspect Theory

Within critical theory, Jürgen Habermas has attempted to establish social theory on the basis of different action orientations which, like the idea of a folk technology, are "quasi-natural" features of human beings everywhere (Habermas 1995: 383). He understands technology as a product of instrumental action, which he opposes to communicative action. Purposive-instrumental reasoning is a feature of all human societies and involves approaching a situation strictly with an eye to the efficient pursuit of a defined objective. This attitude opens out onto a causal analysis of situations that is blind to their significance in any broader sense. The latter is, for Habermas, only brought out if we approach situations with a communicative action orientation. Then we are concerned to share meanings and reach consensus with our fellows. This should be a process that is undistorted by instrumental considerations. In modern societies, these competing action orientations underpin and predominate within two rival social spheres, the system and the lifeworld. Technology, for Habermas, exists within the systems sphere and is not accessible to meaning-orientated interpretation or critique. On this basis, Habermas insists that it is simply an error to try and read meaning into technology (1987: 88–92). When we enter the systems sphere and operate machines, we renounce any concern with meanings and concern ourselves only with the task at hand. This view seems increasingly anachronistic when technology, in the form of mobile phones, PCs and countless other devices, becomes so obviously a part of meaningful cultural life. At the same time, Habermas is surely correct to align technology with a sociologically unproblematic, quasi-universal orientation towards the world.

In contrast, Andrew Feenberg's critical theory of technology is based on a combination of pragmatic and phenomenological approaches to the hermeneutics of technology that incorporates both its instrumental and social dimensions. Feenberg argues that technology is always made up of "neutral" elements and raw materials, which then become incorporated into specific ways of life and social regimes and practices. Technology emerges at the point of intersection between these two things, embodying the knowledge of a particular culture or civilization and the practical requirements of its social organization. Just as the pragmatic position outlined here (cf. Hickman 2001) would suggest, Feenberg insists on the identity of the technological object with both its technical and its social description. He calls this "dual aspect theory" and defines it as follows:

> The technical ideas combined in technology are neutral, but the study of any specific technology can trace in it the impress of a mesh of social determinations which preconstruct a whole domain of social activity aimed at definite goals.
>
> (1991: 81)

Feenberg's theory is intended to handle the antinomy identified earlier as central to the sociologically problematic character of technology. He begins by acknowledging the instrumental character of technical reason, which, following Marcuse, he calls its "problem-solving" orientation. Technology involves concatenations of elements in accordance with rules and these rules are, he implies, based on our scientific understanding of the world. At the same time, which rule sets are to be instantiated in designs is a matter of social choice. It is here that technology is open to social shaping and to power.

In this chapter I have taken John Dewey's definition of technology as denoting a class of objects we experience in their instrumentalities rather than their immediacies as a starting point. Where there is technology we have a physical object that has been modified or constructed in such a way that we can act upon it in order to achieve some effect or change that we would be unable to effect so easily, if at all, in the absence of the technology. This view of technology is criticized by those who see it as superficial and, in particular, as ignoring the significance for society and culture of modern technology. The chapter examined Heidegger's thesis that the idea of technology as instrumentation that enabled humans to realize practical ends was trivial, since it only describes what technology does and not what it is. Technology, on his view, withholds being and serves up practical efficacy instead. As such, it is a kind of substitute for a real life in which experience is valued in itself and meaningful experience is central to human life. In technological culture, he argues, experience is subordinate to the systematized pursuit of ends, which are themselves defined as means to achieve further ends. The romanticism of this view is clear, but I have tried also to draw attention to its extremism. By positioning technology as part of a closed and vicious circle that defines a particular period in history, Heidegger precludes a more dynamic assessment of technology as a historical variable. A more pragmatic approach allows us to see technology as combining culturally universal and more contingent and variable aspects. All societies require some kind of instrumentation if their members are to survive and reproduce. This anthropological premise is not registered by Heidegger. His suspicion of technology is based on the idea that there is a fundamental opposition between meaning, which is the central defining property of humanity, and technology, which endlessly defers matters of content, converting them into practical questions requiring solutions.

When using technology people do not merely glide over the blacked-out surfaces of devices. Part of what makes technology technological is precisely the notion that there is a concealed structure and the inclination to reflect on it. Whoever has travelled by aeroplane has given some thought to the mechanics of flight. Again, there is an analogy with language use. We have all learned language the natural way, from primary socialization processes that have stimulated our grammatical black boxes, cut the neural pathways for language use and so on. We are competent speakers of our native tongue(s). Yet when we come to learn second languages we are more likely to reflect on how language works by looking at the rules of grammar. Similarly, using technology is something we can take for granted much of the time, but it is in the nature of using it that its physical character sometimes obtrudes and we begin to ask how it works. This aspect of our experience with technology defines it as technological. Constructionism correctly emphasizes the fact that people are creative in their use of technology and that their technical inventiveness cannot be separated from the kinds of meaning invested in specific artefacts. However, constructionists have tended to abstract this openness and indeterminacy, which is a feature of technology especially in its early stages, from any notion of the constraints that define it as technology. These involve the necessity of a purpose and of working with known constants in the behaviour of the physical world to achieve that purpose. Just as we all have an interest in making our language use as precise and effective as possible, so when we learn to use a new technology we try and do it properly.

Modernity Theory

Although the previous chapter has made it clear that technology is a universal feature of human societies, there is little doubt that it is particularly salient in cultural modernity. Modern societies have more technologies and they distribute them more widely than pre-modern ones. As Thomas Misa writes, "transport, communication, and merchandising technologies have created a 'modern' experience, and they serve as one long argument for a technological framing of modernity" (Misa *et al.* 2003: 3). Modernity theory describes a culture that differs from traditional human societies by being more productive, rationalized to a greater extent and involving more complex modes of communication and social integration for individuals. Some theorists argue that, while other societies had tools and techniques only modern ones are actually technological. Misa goes so far as to claim that "Technology as a *set* of devices, a complex of industries, or as an abstract force in itself, had yet to appear" (2004: 7) as late as the 1850s. This chapter presents some of the reasons people have thought this way, while at the same time dissenting from a strong identification of technology with modernity. I begin by describing the origins of the notion that technology is distinctively modern in Enlightenment thought of seventeenth-century Europe. A project was initiated at that time of appropriating the idea of effective technology for the European mind. This was mirrored historically by the accumulation of resources through imperial adventures, which meant that the idea of European technological superiority became a self-fulfilling prophecy.

What Misa has in mind when proclaiming the relative novelty of technology is not tools and mechanisms but a substantive social logic which, he thinks, both shapes technology from the second half of the nineteenth century and makes it more ubiquitous and influential on social life. In the sociological tradition, there are three principal ways of grasping this idea of a social rationality that runs through disparate institutions and practices and defines them as modern. Each assigns a central role to technology. For Karl Marx, whose views are discussed in "Production", technology was implicated in the endemic change that seemed to define European societies from the eighteenth century onwards. He argued that this was a contradictory process, in which traditional sources of authority and irrational social prejudice are dissolved by the market and its imperatives while human productive capacity becomes rapidly enlarged. These positive developments are accompanied by the social horrors of industrialism, in which technology is also implicated. In "Rationalization", the idea that modern societies are structured by instrumental or administrative reason is assessed. This view is associated especially with Max Weber and subsequent thinkers within the critical theory tradition who saw it as a necessary supplement to Marx's theories of the economy and social change. Modernity has also been interpreted as involving greater complexity than traditional society. For Durkheim and Mead, the development of modern society involves a differentiation of functions that can be understood on analogy with processes in biological evolution. This tradition informs the critical theory of Jürgen Habermas and is reviewed in "Communication". In "Instrumentalization Theory", I return to Andrew Feenberg, whose thought constitutes an alternative perspective on modernity and technology within social theory. According to his theory of democratic rationalization, technology is complicit in the negative features of modernity, as it is for all the other thinkers described here, but also open to interventions aimed at transforming its meaning for the broader society. In other words, technology can be democratized and recovered as a vehicle for progressive social transformation.

Enlightenment Mythology

In his short story, *New Atlantis*, written in 1620, Francis Bacon describes the arrival of European sailors at a strange island where technology has developed apace. His story gives insights into the place of technology in European thinking about cultural difference and the place of technology in marking out the superiority of some cultures over others. The islanders have discovered techniques for manipulating soil so as to make plants grow without seeds and to be able to convert plants from one species to another; they control the breeding of animals and cultivate hybrid forms for agriculture, and they have developed liquids that can be ingested through the skin, "without all biting, sharpness or fretting" (1905: 729). The islanders tell the sailors, "we have divers mechanical arts, which you have not; and stuffs made by them; as papers linens, silks, tissues; dainty works of feathers of wonderful lustre; excellent dyes, and many others; and shops likewise..." (1905: 729). Using these mechanical arts, the islanders created "perspective-houses, where we make demonstration of all lights and radiations":

> We find also divers means, yet unknown to you, of producing of light origin-ally from divers bodies. We procure means of seeing objects afar off; as in the heaven and remote places; and represent things near as far off, and things afar off as near; making feigned distances. We have also helps for the sight, far above spectacles and glasses in use. We have also glasses and means to see small bodies perfectly and distinctly...
>
> (Bacon 1905: 730)

The islanders have even developed the capacity to simulate tastes and other sensations, so that for entertainment they enjoy time in "houses of deceits of the senses". They have superior engineering, capable of making "faster engines and instruments for all sorts of motions, as well as superior weapons" (1905: 731). There is a strong sense in the story of technology as the future of humanity. When Bacon's sailors enquire about how these achievements were possible they are effectively told that science, as construed by Bacon, and adherence to Christianity are the best route to this envisaged future. Other religious groups, in particular Jews, are present on the island and tolerated, but they are not "like the Jews in other parts" (1905: 724) and homosexuality is not tolerated (But see Jardine and Stewart 1999). The people are orderly so that when they greet the strangers in their midst, "there was never any army that had their men stand in better battle-array" (1905: 726). What we see here is a European thinker assuming owner-ship of technology for himself and his social group. Rival claimants, like women or non-Christians, do not have valid knowledge because they lack the rigour and discipline of the new science. The idea of a distinctive new method for science that would carry us forward was a central pre-occupation of European intellectuals in the seventeenth century. Bacon's story makes it clear how an exaggerated sense of the novelty of scientific method was related to a feeling of superiority over other cultures, a feeling that encompasses issues of social morality and even physical deportment but which starts from a heightened sense of rational procedure. For Bacon in particular, this involved the ascend-ancy of the European mind. Indeed, within Europe itself, the moral authority of science and rationality belonged to those who understood the necessity for a new scientific method. In his 1620, *New Science*, he wrote:

There are and can be only two ways of searching into and discovering truth. The one flies from the senses and particulars to the most general axioms, and from these principles, the truth of which it takes for settled and immoveable, proceeds to judgement and to the discovery of middle axioms. And this way is now in fashion. The other derives axioms from the senses and particulars, rising by a gradual and unbroken ascent, so that it arrives at the most general axioms last of all. This is the true way but yet untried.

(Bacon 1905: 261)

There are a number of problems with this idea that the true way was as yet untried. The first concerns the methodological distinctiveness of European science. Although Bacon was convinced he had discovered a new method for science, it is widely agreed by anthropologists and philosophers of science that the basic reasoning processes characteristic of scientific experimentation and induction are universal traits of the human creature. An abstract procedure, for testing hypotheses or constructing experiments merely formalizes the natural inquisitiveness and intelligence of humans. If anything changes with modernity it is probably less to do with a heightening of the cognitive powers of Europeans than with the circulation of texts and artefacts that enabled people to use their intelligence to greater effect.[1] Much of this traces to the invention of moveable type by Gutenberg in 1450. As Elizabeth Eisenstein (1983) argues, print was important to the development of knowledge not because it catapulted exciting new discoveries all over Europe but primarily because it consolidated established knowledge, combining previously dispersed sources into single publications. Where a scholar might have had to spend a lifetime searching for handwritten sources in disparate locations, print meant that a single purchase secured access to all these sources. Lindberg (1976: 170) shows the importance of this in the history of optics and Kepler's work on the eye. In the early 1500s, the Italian scholar Zerbi printed a work on human anatomy, *Anatomia*, that included 30,000 words summarizing previous studies of the workings of the human eye. There are, apparently, no new ideas in the book. But before it and before print – which is how he came by his sources – such a synthesis and its ready dissemination in a reliable form would have been impossible. This book was read by Johannes Kepler, whose success in the seventeenth century would doubtless have confirmed for Bacon his theory of the power and novelty of scientific method.

Science, including advanced mathematics, astronomy and optics, was well developed elsewhere in the world in the seventeenth century and in previous centuries. In terms of scientific knowledge, early modern Europeans were in many ways inferior to their peers living in other

continents. In his *Machines as the Measure of Men* (1989), Michael Adas
establishes that ideas derived from comparing material, cultural differences, especially technology, were important to how modern Europeans
came to feel superior to people in other continents. Comparisons of technology were present in the accounts of early modern visitors to Africa and
Asia of the thirteenth and fourteenth centuries, but at this time the main
differences they perceived between themselves and the people they met
concerned religion and cultural practices, such as wedding rituals. From
the seventeenth century onwards this began to change, with explorers
comparing their, now improved, navigational and other tools with those
of other cultures. Adas shows that a sense of superiority begins to gather
force from the seventeenth century onwards and comes increasingly to
distort travellers' perceptions with more negative judgements being made
about other cultures in consequence. The idea that other technologies
were inferior and the inference of innate European superiority pre-date
"scientific" racism by at least two centuries. This did not give rise to hard
and fast categorizations of people into specious hierarchies, like those
we find based on race in the nineteenth century (Banton 1986; Malik
1996). But the negative comparison based on technology was probably a
decisive factor in the later emergence of racism. Adas argues that,

> Even in the nineteenth century, when racist theories relating to non-Western
> peoples won their widest acceptance among the articulate [sic] classes of
> Europe, many thinkers gave credence to scientific and technological proofs of
> Western superiority while rejecting those based on racist arguments.
>
> (Adas 1989: 12)

The notion that other people's technology was inferior was initially
expressed in terms of a general doing down of the culture. Consequently,
Chinese society was negatively portrayed as "despotic" and this was
blamed, by Condorcet (1980) and other Enlightenment scholars, for
holding back technological progress. Once other people were defined as
un-technological, a vicious circularity could set in:

> ...a tautological relationship developed: scientific and technological devel-
> opments were frequently cited as gauges of racial capacity, and estimates of
> racial capacity determined the degree of technical and scientific education
> made available to different non-Western peoples.
>
> (Adas 1989: 275)

Consequently, colonial education policy would not even aspire to teach
Africans and Asians science and technology for many years. In this way
the impression was strengthened that they were not interested in or

lacked ability in those subjects. During the centuries of colonial domination, the idea that African and Asian people are inherently technologically inferior, while Europeans are born inventors became a self-fulfilling prophecy.

There is a certain irony to this because the early modern period was in fact one of relative stagnation in European technology and material culture, despite the scientific revolution. Adas comments that between 1450 and 1700 the fork, the fountain pen and cut glass were among the most important things invented in Europe (1989: 28). Meanwhile, Jesuits who actually travelled in Africa provided accounts that falsified the idea of Africa as non-technological, or technologically inferior. Metalworking and superior medical techniques are described by early travellers, including observations like the hinged doors on the homes of the Bayansi people in East Africa. All scholars agree that until the early nineteenth century the material products of China (silks and well-designed artefacts) and India (calico and cotton) were superior to anything in Europe. The fact that even at this time some Europeans were emphasizing the relative complexity of European machines must be taken as indicative of a chauvinism that was to become increasingly powerful. The historical evidence of technological civilization in India before British rule is well known. Zaheer Baber (1996) shows that, notwithstanding the efforts of British thinkers like James Mill to portray it as such, Indian economy and society were not "stagnant" until its major trade routes, internal and external, had been seized by Portuguese and British adventurers during the eighteenth century. The cotton production process had been "technologised" in India – including water-powered cotton gins for making yarn (also used in England until the nineteenth century) – from at least the twelfth century. Moreover, dyeing technologies were advanced in India beyond anything to be found in Europe even into the nineteenth century, when the chemical processes involved began to be understood in European laboratories. Indian steel, called "Wootz", was superior to anything being made in Britain until the advances associated with Cort (in the 1780s) and Bessemer (1850s) became standard, which again was well into the nineteenth century, after European economic dominance had been secured. In military technology, it was Indians who designed metal chambers for firing rockets and these were actually copied by the British (Pacey 1991: 133). In agriculture, from medieval times there were vast irrigation projects including hundreds of kilometres of canals and in the field of medicine as well as developed understanding of herbal medicine (also found in Africa), there is evidence that Indians were inoculating against smallpox in the eighteenth century (Baber 1996: 81). There was also an advanced astronomy in India, although it seems to have been based on geo-centrism, with some developed instrumentation but not telescopes. As the idea of progress took hold[2] in the eighteenth century and played an increasing role in justifying imperialism, it was necessary to construct the historical record in such a way that white Europe came out as the place where genuine innovation and culture could occur. As Martin Bernal puts it: "...after the rise of black slavery and racism, European thinkers were concerned to keep black Africans as far away as possible from European civilization" (1987: 30). This distortion of the truth has affected our understanding of technology as well. The association of technology with the West is an example of a self-fulfilling prophecy. Technology was used by colonial powers to subjugate people who were deliberately kept outside the magic circle of the free exercise of reason. The European countries established their political and economic dominance over other peoples before they enjoyed any military pre-eminence that could be attributed to their technology. They exploited this dominance to undermine and destroy the technological basis of other civilizations, especially in India and Africa, and when new technologies that did have important military applications became available in the nineteenth century they were best placed to invest in them. A decisive turning point in this history came in 1842, when the British used steel-hulled steamships to penetrate deep into Chinese territory (Headrick 1981: 54). The superiority of the "Nemesis" gunship to Chinese craft was then decisive in the British defeat of China. A graphic illustration of the ways in which this dominance has been guarded even in recent times is provided by the exclusion of Russian, Japanese and Indian scientists, including Einstein's collaborator and co-author Homi Bhabba, from British work on nuclear weapons (Pacey 1991: 178). The struggle for strategic dominance secured through possession of advanced military technologies continues to be a source of controversy in the world today, as states that already have nuclear weapons, and in some cases are in the process of up-grading them, try to prevent others from obtaining nuclear technology.

Production

As Don Ihde has pointed out (1990: 30–1), it was through Marx's intervention that the question of technology first imposed itself on philosophy and theoretical reflection. Marx assigns technology, which he usually refers to as the productive forces of society, an explanatory role in relation to all historical development. Marx retained from Enlightenment, and his Victorian social context, the idea that technological change was fundamentally progressive. However, he also emphasized that technology as it was being developed by capitalism entailed suffering and misery for the vast majority of the people who had to work with it. According to Marx, what makes technology progressive is not the fact that it embodies a special kind of reasoning but its capacity to enhance productive power. If human history is thought of as a structure or a building, technology is the foundational level that supports the rest. Moreover, technology has an in-built tendency to develop and become more efficient, so that human beings can produce more useable goods from fewer inputs, measured in terms of expended labour and raw materials used (Cohen 1978). This means that other layers of the historical process are obliged to change and from this we can derive the dynamic character of human history. In his most famous comment on technology, Marx assigns the productive forces a central explanatory role:

> In the social production of their existence, men inevitably enter into definite relations, which are independent of their will, namely relations of production appropriate to a given stage in the development of their material forces of production. The totality of these relations constitutes the economic structure of society, the real foundation on which there arises a legal and political superstructure and to which correspond definite forms of social consciousness.
>
> (Marx 1972: 20)

In this comment, especially the emphasis on social arrangements as "independent" of our will, Marx suggests that law, politics and even our ideas about the world are effects of the need to make collective adjustments to the presence of specific kinds of technology. However, Marx's theory of technology is not determinist. Marx tells us repeatedly that in his philosophy, human beings make history, albeit not under conditions of their own choosing.[3] They are not told what direction to move in by an impersonal force that they cannot control. On the contrary, in *Capital*, Marx placed technology at the centre of the historical process in a much more interesting and suggestive way. There he wrote that,

> Technology discloses man's mode of dealing with Nature, the process of production by which he sustains his life, and thereby also lays bare the mode of formation of his social relations, and of the mental conceptions that flow from them.
>
> (1983: 352)

From this it is clear that Marx understands technology as a human, social creation. By studying it we can find out about the human beings who created it – their understanding of nature, their forms of social organization and their broader beliefs. Interpretation of technology reveals crucial social properties. It is not external to the historical process but is formed as a part of the social practices that make history happen. Analysis of technology that is guided by these comments will need to take on board the significance technology has for its designers, the meanings it has for its users and its many-sided relationship to culture and ideas. By bringing technology firmly within the compass of social analysis and critique, Marx was able to criticize industrial technology, while still maintaining that technology as a whole played the progressive function he assigned to it in the *1859 Preface* and elsewhere.

The key technology of modernity, according to Marx was the steam engine. James Watt's "second and so-called double-acting steam engine", which he patented in 1784 as "an agent universally applicable in Mechanical Industry" (Marx 1983: 357), made the industrial revolution possible.[4] Steam powered artefacts had been used for centuries prior to this – Boorstin (1985) writes of their use in Ancient Greece – and Watt's device was really a modification of the Newcomen engine, used for decades as a pump. Watt's design made the engine more efficient and enabled it to generate rotary motion (Fichman 1993: 100–2). This made it more versatile so that it could be used in a range of production processes, from milling corn to spinning cotton. The productive potential of this device was seized upon by capitalists from the late eighteenth century. What comes across most clearly in Marx's writings on industrial technology is the sheer dynamism of capitalist development. The rise of the market mechanism as principal arbiter of value in human affairs undermines traditional sources of authority. People must negotiate and manoeuvre to secure survival in a market where we are all only worth what someone will pay for our services. Feudal peasants were dependent and deferential in relation to their masters but they also claimed security from their attachment to a particular plot of land, a social function they had for life and a set of religious views that did not change. All this is swept aside by capitalist modernity, as Marx and Engels describe in the *Communist Manifesto*:

> Constant revolutionising of production, uninterrupted disturbance of all social conditions, everlasting uncertainty and agitation distinguish the bourgeois epoch from all earlier ones. All fixed, fast-frozen relationships, with their train of ancient and venerable prejudices and opinions are swept away, all new-formed ones become antiquated before they can ossify. All that is solid melts into air, all that is holy is profaned, and man is at last compelled to face with sober sense, his real conditions of life and his relations with his kind.
>
> (Marx and Engels 1967: 83)

The difference is symbolized for Marx by the very buildings of the new capitalist centres, the cities of nineteenth-century Europe. Structures as large as medieval cathedrals (built to last for millennia) could be erected and pulled down again within a decade by profit-hungry entrepreneurs armed with powerful industrial technologies (Berman 1982). No structure is permanent since capitalism constantly revolutionizes the means of social production in the pursuit of competitive advantage. With its "unceasing improvement of machinery" (Marx 1967: 89) capitalism makes rapid technological change normal.

According to Marx, human society must pass through a number of historical stages corresponding to levels in the development of the productive forces. Socialism – the first fair society, in which each person receives the goods they need to realize their own inner potential – requires an enormously powerful productive base, for obvious reasons. Because Marx believed that history was developing productive forces sufficient for this purpose, he was able to remain optimistic about the process as a whole, despite his detailed knowledge of the horrors of nineteenth-century industrial capitalism. A pressing problem for this view, when Marx was writing, was the active use of technology by imperialist powers, especially Britain, to dominate people in other parts of the world. These policies were justified by their apologists in terms of a civilizing mission that was bringing the benefits of technological progress to parts of the world that would otherwise have been sunk in some kind of pre-technological barbarism. Although he castigated British imperialism for exploiting India, Marx seems not to have broken with this, perhaps the prevailing idea of his time, which cast Europe as leading the way in science and technology, with other parts of the world falling in behind. For this reason, Michael Adas (1989: 241) suggests that Marx is guilty of euro-centrism. The reasoning behind the accusation is clear: Marx seems to think that (industrial) technology is a European invention; he believes it's (ultimately) a good thing and, therefore, he endorses the cultural superiority of Europe – its "leading role".

In a similar vein, Zaheer Baber (1996: 209–10) argues that Marx betrays cultural bias in his writings on the Indian railways. In early writings, Marx was enthusiastic about the imperial authorities' project of constructing a rail network across India. He saw this as progressive because, "the railway system will become . . . the forerunner of modern industry" and therefore be the key to progress in India. Years later, however, Marx wrote that the railways were "useless to the Hindus" and lamented the fact that the construction costs were being paid from a levy being raised on the Indians by the British. At this point it seemed to Marx as if the rail connections merely facilitated rapid extraction of cotton for British mill owners, rather than providing India with a useful transportation infrastructure. Baber argues that this shows Marx's early faith in progress – his belief that technology must ultimately be beneficial – incorporated a belief that the

European model of capitalist development was the most desirable course
for India. In other words, Marx's belief that technologically enhanced
productive capacity is the guiding principle of historical development
led him to neglect other values that might be realized, possibly through
different uses of technology. Marx identified the contradictions in the
social context that led the British Empire to bequeath India railways, but
was unable to see that this contradiction extended to the design of the
technology itself. Endorsing the European capitalist model of technological development led Marx to neglect value systems other than the
one that emphasizes human freedom through greater material wealth.
Such values constrained technology development in other cultures in the
pre-Modern era. Elites in India and Japan, for example, suppressed development of spinning and military technologies, respectively, to preserve
institutions that might have been imperilled by such changes (Baber
1996; Jansen 2002). However, from any sensible normative vantage point,
improvements in transportation are a good thing and in this sense Marx's
early, positive appraisal is not straightforwardly wrong. Writing a few
decades after Marx in the 1890s, Horace Bell reported that, while colonial
planners had created a railway for moving goods rather than people,
by then the value of passenger traffic far exceeded that of goods (Bell
1894: 4). Subsequent generations had seized upon affordances in the
railway system and adapted it to economic and social purposes that
could not have been anticipated by colonial planners. Whether the Indian
railway has benefited Indian society and whether another design would
have benefited it more are open questions not susceptible of straightforward answers.

I think that Marx's theory is not culturally chauvinist, but is committed
to the idea that science and technology, as the embodiment of our
improving knowledge of and leverage over the world could not, in principle, be regressive. This is only chauvinistic if we accept that science
and technology development are European values.[5] The historical record,
however, shows that technology was not a European achievement. As
we have seen, similar technologies are developed by humans working
in different cultural contexts. What Pacey (1999) calls "survival" technologies are developed by people everywhere to solve similar kinds of
problem. This is not to deny the availability of different technological
paths, but it does imply that they share a common foundation in the
anthropologically given needs and interests of the human creature. Marx's
emphasis on production is intended to grasp this and, viewed in this way,
the positive goal of technology development cannot be seen as limited
to any particular cultural worldview.

Moreover, Marx's vision of socialism is a society whose central value
is freedom and this is not consistent with the elitist and religious social

institutions that were used to check technology development in traditional societies. For him, enlarging the scope of individual autonomy is indexical for social progress and is not a culturally relative value. It is possible that upholding freedom might entail limiting certain kinds of technology development. A good case can be made for this in connection with nuclear power, for example, since the waste products might necessitate a security apparatus whose mode of organization is incompatible with a free way of life (cf. Winner 1980). The point here, though, is that such containment needs to be justified rationally and through public discourse. The romantic idea that technology as whole might need to be inhibited – as when Greens and others polemicize against "technological fix" solutions – in defence of a romanticized conception of nature, or aesthetic values not essential to freedom, is incompatible with Marx's view. Having said this, it must be acknowledged that Marx's faith in technological development seems to have been inherited from the European Enlightenment and that in his emphasis on material production he failed to reflect on the culturally selected range of alternative routes for technology development, freed from the constraints of elitist political systems and cultures, to take.

Rationalization

Max Weber was the first social theorist to comprehend the notion of an historically distinctive, pervasive modern rationality. Weber (1974) concurs with the Enlightenment scholars that scientific reasoning sets us free from tradition, eroding deference to religious authority for example, but sees that it also constitutes a trap for modern subjects. According to his account, what he called "purposive-instrumental" action begins to override other ways of deliberating over and understanding one's own actions from the seventeenth century onwards. This means that increasingly we assess our actions only in terms of whether they deliver our desired outcomes, without regard for their intrinsic rightness or their ultimate (perhaps religious) significance. As philosopher Richard J. Bernstein puts it, Weber tried to show that this kind of reasoning extended to "virtually every domain of modern culture and society – including science, morality, law, politics, economics, administration, bureaucracy, even the arts" in modernity and that it "shapes every aspect of our daily lives" (Bernstein 1991: 40).

Formal, instrumental reasoning leaves us in a hollowed-out world in which means have supplanted ends and attachment to method displaces any concern with meaning. What characterizes modernity, Weber argues, is that we are trapped in a cage of rationality, with no obvious escape route. He uses the metaphor of "mechanical petrifaction" to convey the sense that by instrumentalizing our actions in the pursuit of efficiency we have effectively deprived ourselves of any reason for acting in the first place. Weber's thesis is that modernity is the cultural experience of abstraction; it is life in a uniquely ordered, regimented society in which formal rule-following overrides any attachment to substantive principles or values that are not susceptible to rational, scientific analysis. Although Weber did not write about clocks, the mechanical clock was the technology that made his modernity possible.

Mechanical, weight-driven clocks began appearing in the town squares of Europe from the beginning of the fourteenth century (Landes 1983; Mayr 1986). They were first used in monasteries, where they enabled monks to pray on-schedule. According to David S. Landes, before about 1600 they were not intrinsically more accurate or reliable than water clocks or even sundials. However, mechanical clocks did hold out specific affordances that those devices lacked. They were usable in all weathers, inherently more portable and they could be miniaturized (Landes 1983: 66). As Landes points out, though, it was not inevitable that these potentials would be realized: "The clock did not create an interest in time measurement; the interest in time measurement led to the invention of the clock" (1983: 58). Ultimately, it was the convergence of the clock with the interests of the burgeoning capitalist class and a system of production based on co-ordination of large numbers of workers, who from the eighteenth century would be summoned to work by the chime of a mechanical clock in a public space, that drove the development of the technology.[6] At the same time, the salience of clocks impacted upon the culture:

> That the mechanical clock did appear in the West, and with it a civilization organized around the measurement and knowledge of time, is a critical factor in the differentiation of the West from the Rest and the rise of Europe to technological and economic hegemony.
>
> (Landes 1983: 25)

Clocks made possible a new sense of time as something abstract and uniform where previously there had only been lived time with its rhythms and flows corresponding to natural cycles and cultural sensations. For critic of modernity Lewis Mumford the change was technologically determined: "by its essential nature ... [the clock] dissociated time from human events and helped create the belief in an independent world of fundamentally measurable sequences" (Mumford 1947: 15). In fact, clocks enabled Europeans to co-ordinate their activities much more tightly than other societies and this affordance, alongside other changes, made societal rationalization possible.

Weber's theory informed a romantic view of technology in twentieth-century critical theory. For thinkers of the Frankfurt School the role played by technology in the domination of some social groups by others is not traceable to the alliance of science and capitalism from the nineteenth century onwards, but has its origins in science as a way of relating to the natural physical world. For Adorno and Horkheimer, the attitude of looking at things in order to secure leverage over them always involves a kind of violence. At the origins of human civilization, they argue, there is an urge to dominate nature.[7] This urge is manifest in calculative reasoning, which they characterize as cold and illuminating. Scientific reason does violence to things because it can only see mathematical quantities and order in them. In essence, they say, the scientific mind deposits itself in things, reducing them all to the same status. It then discovers itself in the world and in so doing neglects all the other possibilities that the world held open. Whereas Heidegger and others, as we have seen, associate this kind of foreclosing of the possibilities in the world specifically with modern, industrial technology, Adorno and Horkheimer argue that,

> The lines from reason, liberalism and the bourgeois spirit go incomparably further back than historians who date the notion of the burgher only from the end of medieval feudalism would allow.
>
> (Adorno and Horkheimer 1979: 45)

The violence of modern societies has its origins in a particular way of knowing things, which is scientific and which gives rise to capitalism and technology. According to this view, "the deductive form of science reflects hierarchy and coercion" (1979: 21) and these have been present throughout human history. In capitalist modernity, they intensify and what is particularly regrettable about the modern period is not so much that we have these things at all as that, from the Enlightenment onwards, they become the only ways of approaching the world that are sanctioned as legitimate, leading to knowledge in the case of science and to freedom from natural constraints in the form of technology.

In his critique of pragmatism, Horkheimer betrays the conservative orientation of this version of critical theory. He identifies the early Enlightenment period in sixteenth-century Europe as a time when scientific reason began to displace religion as the basis for new social institutions like the sovereign city state and, whereas other commentators (for example, Skinner 1992; Sassen 2006) identify this as a period that heralds the dawn of democracy and citizenship as central values of modernity, Horkheimer claims there is already an incipient fascism. Behind the appearance of reason and debate, he sees an enhanced role for manipulation. Reason "had come to signify a conciliatory attitude" and,

> ... was doubtless more humane but at the same time weaker than the religious concept of truth, more pliable to prevailing interests, more adaptable to reality as it is, and therewith from the beginning, in danger of surrendering to the irrational.

(1974: 13)

The fundamental weakness of reason was its vulnerability to "formaliz-ation" (1974: 36). While reason should be about attempting to reach the truth based on a sincere and interest-free approach, in reality it becomes distorted into a tool of power. Horkheimer argues that this is what has happened to pragmatism, which, he says, "reflects a society that has no time to remember and meditate" (1974: 44). Pragmatism cannot accom-modate transcendent values and insists on asking about the utility of ideas, or their function in maintaining social order, rather than acknow-ledging the possibility of a higher truth. Horkheimer's caricature of prag-matism is of only passing interest, but its implication for technology is clear. "Only under ideal harmonious conditions could progressive histor-ical changes be brought about by the authority of science" (1974: 83) and one of the social factors that menaces that harmony is the tendency to formalize reason and to make it work without regard to ultimate values. Since, as we have seen, technology is instrumentality; it is embodied and formalized reason without intrinsic ends, it must be forever excluded from consideration in the higher realms of critical theory. The Marxist idea that technology, while ambivalent, is an agent for social progress gives way to an intellectual defence of humanity that excludes this part of human endeavour as somehow beneath it. Ironically, there is a latent fascism in Horkheimer's own position, since it seems that, for him, only those tools, activities and games that uphold and project the orientation to a higher truth can ever be valid. Technology here is completely implic-ated in the substantive social logic of modernity, which is instrumental reason. For Adorno and Horkheimer, capitalist modernity unleashes tech-nology to secure its productive gains, but the result is a society in which considerations of value and meaning are menaced by instrumentalism. Later thinkers in the critical theory tradition, especially Andrew Feenberg, have attempted to rescue technology from this negative position and at the same time to rework Weber's notion of societal rationalization as a process that presents opportunities as well as dangers. I return to this below.

Communication

The third strand within modernity theory to be discussed here also takes its lead from strains in Enlightenment thinking and argues that what defines modern societies is their increased complexity relative to traditional societies. This complexity requires individuals to reflect on how their actions comport with the expectations of society as a whole. Members of traditional society were integrated unreflectively into stable systems of meaning that were not challenged or subject to revision. The endemic change associated with modernity means that finding one's place becomes increasingly a matter for individuals (Durkheim 1964). Whereas for Enlightenment thinkers the differentiation of science was unambiguously progressive,[8] Mead understood it in more evolutionary terms. The problem of technological change becomes that of maintaining the functional integration of individuals into a social world that is de-stabilized by rapid changes and bereft of the reassurances of traditional authority. In other words, the problem of modernity is that society itself must be kept on a healthy developmental course despite its tendency towards convulsions caused by things like technological innovation and increases in complexity of social organization. On the other hand, societies with a more developed technological basis flow from social conditions in which individuals are free to think and experiment for themselves. This positive development presupposes human individuals who have learned from their formative socialization how to be independent of society, while remaining aware that it has formed them. As the pragmatist philosopher and social psychologist G.H. Mead put it, "A person is a personality because he belongs to a community, because he takes over the institutions of that community into his own conduct" (1967: 162). An appropriate balance of individuation and integration is optimal both for the cultivation of human individuals and for vibrant and prosperous societies. Technology takes its place in this picture. According to Mead, "Speech and the hand go together in the development of the social human being" (1967: 237), by which he means that learning to act effectively and learning to communicate in the language of one's fellows are both key to becoming a person. The first includes technology use and both this and communicative competence are central to being an integrated member of any society. A society progresses, however, only in so far as the form taken by its technology and by its cultural media for self-expression continue to be consistent with the balance between individuation and integration. A society in which people had similar opinions on most matters, or in which there was little communication between members would no longer be involved in the "process of development" as understood by Mead (1967: 252).

Viewed in terms of this emphasis on integration and a shared sense of belonging to communities, modern societies are uniquely possessed of communications technologies, the most important of which was print. By 1500 there were print shops in every municipal centre in Europe. Before print, books were copied by hand and some religious orders encouraged copying as a devotional discipline. However, the situation of texts reproduced in this way was precarious. There was a dynamic at the heart of scribal culture, whereby wider circulation menaced preservation – which encouraged secrecy. But at the same time, a fire in a library might destroy the only copy of an ancient tome. Printing made more copies of a book possible. This in turn ensured they were present in social space in a new way. Once print arrived it was no longer necessary, if you wanted to own a book, to copy it all out for yourself. While there may have been anxiety about the fate of copying as a devotional activity, this did not give rise to significant resistance from clerics. Many of the monks and nuns who had been copyists became printers and monasteries became print works, producing religious tracts. The fact that reliable copies of books could be obtained for money meant that scholars no longer had to spend time at the feet of their masters, learning from them and copying books for them. Before print, scholars might spend years mastering one or two sources in detail. Now they could read several books in a short period of time. Scholarly activity acquired a new mobility and freedom.

Media theorists have argued that typographical fixity made possible a completely different psychology of learning. This was the psychology of the lone reader – the person who gathers information about the world silently, by ingesting details from the printed page that is in front of him or her alone. He or she no longer relies on the words of a preacher or orator to tell him or her what is going on. This feeds into the development of Protestantism too, since that movement was essentially a reaction against the role of Priests who, according to Catholicism, mediate between us and God. Reading the bible at home you can feel God's word speaking to you from within, you do not need an intermediary. This is the basic psychology behind Lutheranism and Calvinism, studied by Weber (1974). It is a short step from finding out about the world for one's self to calculating what one's own interests are and how they might be advanced. In this way, the new psychology underscored a new "public" or political orientation. Historian Elizabeth Eisenstein writes that, "even while communal solidarity was diminished, vicarious participation in more distant events was also enhanced; and even while local ties were loosened, links to larger collective units were being forged" (Eisenstein 1983: 94; see also Thompson 1995). For the first time it became possible and even normal for people to identify with social and political causes without ever meeting anyone with direct personal involvement in them. A new sphere opened up in which people act on the basis of this depersonalized, even abstract information. Taken together, these developments constitute the mass psychological basis of what the second wave Frankfurt School theorist Jürgen Habermas calls the "public sphere". Only through the agency of print (a communications technology) does it become possible for people to think of themselves as members of an "imagined community", the basis of modern nationalism (Anderson 1983, C.3). Like the steam engine and the clock, print presented affordances to modern societies that were explained in ways that reflected the social and cultural situation. Specific cultural logics were then amplified by the new technologies, culminating in a "tipping point" (Sassen 2006), after which cultural modernity becomes an identifiable social and cultural formation.

Building on insights from Durkheim and especially Mead, Habermas argues (1979, 1989) that modern societies are premised on novel socialization processes that give modern individuals access to distinctive new capabilities. Through mass literacy and the spread of print media subjects are formed for whom membership of an imagined community on a national scale is almost second nature. This identification of one's self with a bigger picture is peculiarly modern partly as a function of its scale but also because it is associated with a new distance of each subject from traditional sources of authority and meaning. Modern individuals have a stronger sense of themselves as independent agents with choices than peoples of an earlier age. Participation in the public sphere is one way in which such individuals secure integration with society and regain a sense of themselves as members of a community with common values. To achieve this we use the resources of what Habermas (1995) calls the "cultural lifeworld", of which literacy is a key element. Habermas sees an analogy between the ways in which healthy individuals grow psychologically to maturity and the development of stable societies – an analogy that was also important to Enlightenment scholars like Condorcet and Turgot, who were discussed above (see Strydom 1992). Societies, he says, are subject to the same developmental pattern as human individuals and are prone to analogous breakdowns and pathologies. Just as healthy individuals learn to differentiate their roles and to compartmentalize different functions within manageable levels of complexity, so societies differentiate themselves into separate spheres, within which there is further division consistent with the overall well-being of the social organism. In modern societies, this involves the historical separation of the system from the cultural lifeworld (Habermas 1995; for discussion see Baxter 1987; Johnson 1991). As we saw at the end of the previous chapter, this split, which is characteristic of modern societies, accommodates human

beings' capacity for instrumental action on the world, including technology, within the systems sphere. This is the dimension of social evolution
within which economic activity occurs and, in Habermas's model, it is
uncluttered by questions of meaning or value. Progress here is measured
in terms of output and efficiency. The other sphere, the lifeworld, is the
realm of culture and meaning. Here people create and share objects and
ideas which define what it feels like to live in their culture. They strive to
reach agreement on the major ethical issues that confront them collect-
ively and they forge lives that are individually fulfilling, based on their
own personal beliefs concerning ultimate ends and values. Progress here
is measured negatively in terms of the avoidance of pathologies associated with the breakdown of individuality, failures of integration and loss
of cultural meaning.

Habermas argues that the systems sphere can become overdeveloped
and threaten processes essential to the maintenance of a viable lifeworld
a process he calls colonization. Technology is implicated because what
Habermas has in mind is that technical or instrumental reasoning might
encroach upon areas of life that should really be the preserve of what he
calls "communicative reason". Reflective discourse that decides between
values and assesses the significance of actions can be displaced in favour
of a "technocratic" approach to policy (the latter can refer to matters
of personal life as well as institutional politics). Where this happens,
the evolutionary stability of society is imperilled, raising the prospect of
pathological developments. Habermas's concern is not with technology
as a mode of human action per se, which he understands as quasi-
natural, but with the inappropriate use of instrumental reasoning to solve
problems that involve meaning and value. However, the system/lifeworld
distinction abstracts technology from society. In consequence, Habermas
actually regresses behind Marx. Indeed, Marx observed that bourgeois
economists of his time, who supported the development of the factory
system as progress would at the same time be opposed to regulation
of the economy: "It is very characteristic that the enthusiastic apologists of the factory system have nothing more damning to urge against
a general organisation of the labour of society, than that it would turn
all society into one immense factory" (Marx 1983: 337). The comparison
is harsh, but it does seem that Habermas endorses a systems sphere
based on mindless conformity while he is worried at the prospect of it
spreading beyond what is "necessary". Habermas's distinction between
system and lifeworld is strictly analytical; he acknowledges that in practice the two spheres interpenetrate. However, the separation of system
and lifeworld conjoins technology, in its pragmatic foundation, so to
speak, to a permanent association with coercive authority and makes it
inherently opposed to reason and communication, which are construed

as radically distinct from technology. Yet print is also technology and novel configurations of the social and technical, to be discussed further in subsequent chapters, have become central to the logic of capitalist development since the 1980s. To comprehend this changed situation we need to re-assess the place of technology in relation to instrumental reason, as formulated in classical social and critical theory, as the dominant social rationality.

Instrumentalization Theory

Andrew Feenberg has argued that Habermas is wrong to limit technology to the systems sphere in this way. Technology is also about communication and the enrichment of cultural life and so in our assessment of a given technology design we are justified in asking about more than its capacity to enhance our productivity. New designs should be assessed for the ways in which they play into our social relationships and their impact on the cultural and institutional context of democratic decision-making. According to Feenberg, the emphasis on productive efficiency, which we also find in Marx, is a contingent value, even a distortion of our perception of technology. Developing new technologies and designing artefacts that change our lives in ways that have nothing to do with efficiency or the instrumental pursuit of profit can be part of a political project that aims to counter the pernicious influence of capitalist, market-based principles in social and cultural life. His idea of a progressive "technical politics" involves challenging the hegemony of capitalist assumptions about what is desirable and about what constitutes "good" technology design.

To understand Feenberg's intervention it is useful to rehearse an argument of his teacher, Herbert Marcuse, who was associated with the first generation of Frankfurt scholars. Like Adorno and Horkheimer, Marcuse associated technology with an original violence that appropriates objects from their original position in the world and strips them down to reveal their usefulness for human society. However, he maintained that while current technology was instrumental and therefore regressive, the possibility remained of an alternative technical stance that would be consistent with the Frankfurt School's critique of science. He speculated that the way out of the "totally administered society", which he called "one-dimensional" would be through a revolution led not by workers but by advocates of this alternative technology. Marcuse connects the concerns of critical theory with Heidegger's idea of modern, capitalist technology as enframing and argues that, " . . . when the technical becomes the universal form of material production, it circumscribes an entire culture; it projects a historical totality – a 'world' " (Marcuse 1964: 154). At present, technical and formalized rationality are the main vehicles for reification and ideology, that is, for irrationality: "the rational rather than the irrational becomes the most effective vehicle of mystification" (1964: 189). Technocracy replaces democracy as we seek instrumental "solutions" to all our collective dilemmas, themselves now defined as "problems". The extent to which social irrationality has compromised technology development itself means that political change can only be brought about through the development of new technologies that subvert capitalist technocracy from within. In this way, the historical function of technology as the "pacification of the struggle for existence" (1964: 227) could be reclaimed and completion of the technological project can result in transcendence of the technological society. Marcuse's vision is of a technology that is not shaped and defined by capitalist interests and the social logic of instrumental, or disciplinary reason. We have seen that, for modernity theorists, this is difficult to envisage because technology and modernity are so thoroughly implicated in one another. Indeed, Thomas Misa was cited at the start of this chapter asserting they were inextricably entangled.

Feenberg has addressed this question through his theory of primary and secondary instrumentalization. For Feenberg, as for earlier Frankfurt School theorists, technology is the result of an original violence against nature that lies at the heart of technical reason. He calls this "primary instrumentalisation" and what he has in mind is Marcuse's idea that there is violence in the act by which things are removed from their natural settings and repositioned so as to take on utility for human beings with an instrumental attitude towards them. In what Feenberg calls "normal" (2002: 177) technology development, the violence of primary instrumentalization is compensated for by a second moment in the development of an artefact, which is secondary instrumentalization. Here the artefact, having been pulled from its natural setting is re-contextualized. Investments of value and meaning are placed in the object so that it takes on a restored significance; its new place in the world is not as a violated object but as bearer of positive value for people. Normal societies integrate these two moments, so that the carpenter, for example, decorates his tools with flutes and engravings.[9] The utility of the object is matched by a corresponding aestheticization that, along with instrumental practice, helps assign it a new status in the world. Feenberg argues that this dialectical model of technology combines the critical insights of earlier approaches[10] with Marcuse's desire for technology as part of a "redeemed modernity" (2002: 176).

By distinguishing primary and secondary instrumentalization, Feenberg is able to show that, understood as an ambivalent phenomenon, technology is actually stymied in its development by capitalism:

> The dialectic of technology is short-circuited under capitalism in one especially important domain: the technical control of the labour force. Special obstacles to secondary instrumentalisation are encountered wherever integrative technical change would threaten that control ... [T]he integration of skill and intelligence into production is often arrested by the fear that the firm will become dependent on its workers ... The critical theory of technology exposes the obstacles to the release of technology's integrative potential and thus serves as the link between technical and political discourse.
>
> (2002: 177)

The history of technology being used to control labour over the past few centuries is a miserable one that involves significant moments of normative regret. For Feenberg this history discloses an ethical danger specific to technology. When we exploit instrumentalities in the physical–natural world this can be problematic, but when we treat other human beings in this way, it is inherently troubling. In pre-capitalist cultures, such a perspective on fellow humans is always contained in some cultural packaging, so that treating someone as an object in an instrumental series of events is invested with symbolic significance, normally at some cost to the person benefiting from that series of events, that makes the loss of humanity acceptable, perhaps meaningful to all parties. What characterizes modernity is, in Bruno Latour's phrase, "indifference to the consequences" of such instrumental actions, even when they involve other people. Only capitalist modernity allows technical or instrumental use of other human beings without any such compensating process, symbolic or otherwise. However, I believe the history of technology's use against labour under capitalism may be distorting Feenberg's perspective here. The lack of moral concern for others that we find in capitalist societies and not the instrumental attitude towards them is what is morally regrettable. A technical ordering of a process or set of relations is a matter for regret only when it is actually part of a process that involves the domination – through systematic disadvantage or actual abuse – of a person. Some instrumentalized social processes do not involve this, as when workplaces are engineered to maintain employees' self-esteem to maximize productivity. Moreover, there are abuses of neglect, often in domestic and caring situations that are devoid of any relevant technical dimension. Finally, the history of work and of the use of power in what we may call uncompensated cruelty is not peculiarly modern. Slaves sent to the silver mines of Ancient Athens, for example, did not survive more than five years and were, in a social sense, invisible.[11] The point is that there is no intrinsic association of normative regret or immoral domination with instrumental or technical reason as applied to human affairs. They add nothing to a pragmatic understanding of technology as artefacts produced through interaction with the world guided by a practical focus on means.

In primary instrumentalization, we can see the sensible, Habermasian idea of technology as a strategic action orientation that is part of the historically available repertoire of action orientations for the human animal. Hence at one point Feenberg cites breast-feeding as an example (1999: 173). But in Feenberg's development of it we can also detect the idea of a fearful violence that separates us from nature and terminates a kind of integrated harmony with the environment. Hence, he suggests a deep affinity between it and the violence implicit in capitalism (1999: 91). In this prevarication over whether primary instrumentalization is inherently violent or in fact neutral, Feenberg concedes too much to substantivist definitions of technology.[12] He argues that in "normal" societies secondary instrumentalization corrects the violence of primary instrumentalization with culturally variable instruments of meaning. Under capitalism, however, secondary instrumentalization becomes merely an amplification of the violence towards nature (human and environmental) implicit in primary instrumentalization. Modern, capitalist societies see a massive escalation in the quantity of technology, but a drastic scaling down of its social meaning. Technology becomes more narrowly instrumental and less meaningful so that, as we get more of it, we are more exposed to its inherent violence. The possibility of an alternative secondary instrumentalization is the opening for a Marcusian counter to this situation and involves what Feenberg calls a "re-aestheticisation" of technology design. I will return to this idea in Chapter 6.

It is important for critical theory to get away from the idea that cultural modernity produces technology that is distinguished by its uniquely unnatural or anti-natural character. All societies have technology and artifice and they all combine this with a high degree of cultural inventiveness and produce the meanings that are essential to collective life, in the sense described in Chapter 2. It is very difficult, if not impossible, to stipulate that any one historical society is, in its rhythms, its pace of life or other aspects of its organization any more or less "natural" or "closer to nature" than any other. Consequently, I think we have to take issue with Adas when he writes that,

> ... the Europeans who explored, colonised and sought to Christianise Africa and Asia were setting out from societies dominated by clocks, railway schedules, and mechanical rhythms. They "went out" to cultures still closely attuned to the cycles of nature, to societies in which leisure was savoured, patience

was highly regarded, and everyday life moved at a pace that most Western intruders found enervating if not downright exasperating.

(1989: 243)

Clocks gave Europeans a distinctive sense of time and enabled certain strategies in relation to time that became fundamental to European domination (1989: 209). But Adas suggests in these comments that Europeans had clock time and Africans and others "still" had an unmediated, more natural time and rhythm. It seems to me that this may itself be evidence of, albeit benign cultural prejudice. African societies were co-ordinated and integrated entities involving the active participation of thousands of people (Ranger 1992: 248). This would simply not be possible without some principles of organization and some order in the temporal dimension of social life. It is difficult to imagine a human society that does not measure time and record it in some way. Although Mayr maintains (1986: 15) that mechanical clocks do not meet any basic human need, this is not true – they meet the basic need for time keeping in a way that presents capabilities and affordances that were not available in their absence. The need for calendar like measurement operations applied to longer stretches of time was asserted in the previous chapter and it is clear that all societies require some conventions relating to time if they are to solve elementary co-ordination problems. The point about mechanical clocks is that they meet that need in a specific way that opens up new affordances, not that they are uniquely "technological". Some of Adas's comments on mechanical clocks are suggestive, but this change of technological style, affecting the rhythm of life should not be opposed to a "more natural" way of living in time associated with "pre-clock" societies. As Adas knows well, all societies employ technological means for recording the passage of time, ranging from water clocks to sundials. This is an elementary technological function and it is always associated with the imposition of cultural routine upon background, natural temporalities.

We have seen that technology is not unique to cultural modernity and that other cultures also included efficient and specialized technologies. What defines cultural modernity, then, is not its technological character but rather the specific intersection of social, economic and cultural factors of early modern Europe, associated with capitalism, with specific new technologies. These technologies did not cause revolutionary change but they held out affordances or potentials that were exploited and developed in specific directions under the social conditions of Europe at that time. Hence, printing presses, clocks and steam engines became powerful factors working for the emergence of a new distinctive social formation but they did so only as they were themselves developed and their affordances selectively unlocked by social forces. Marx's insight that the fundamental dynamic here was the emergence of an economy based on markets and shaking off the cultural constraints set by pre-capitalist elites remains the best starting point for a synthesis of these insights. Science, technology and instrumentalism as a basic orientation are developed in particular ways by capitalism, perhaps even distorted by it, but they are universal features of the human animal and cannot themselves be viewed as the source of modernity's ills or usefully contrasted with the tools of a more "natural" way of life.

Social Domination

4

Previous chapters have suggested some ways in which technology has been implicated in historical social power relationships. This chapter will clarify what power means in this context. Following Lukes (2005), I will suggest that using the idea of power always involves making a normative judgement about an event or a situation. When we speak of power we suggest that things could have been otherwise in its absence and we invite reflection on whether that alternative state of affairs might have been preferable. In this chapter, I attempt to clarify when it is appropriate to approach technology in this way. A central objective of the chapter is to make clear the circumstances under which critical social theory ought to be concerned with technology and why. I argue that it can be meaningful and worthwhile to make a sociological critique of technology but that technology is not necessarily at the centre of critical theory's concerns – something which tends to be taken for granted by theorists who embrace the association of cultural modernity with technology. This involves setting some limits on the scope and objectives of critique itself, as well as further refinements of the notion of what technology is and the extent to which its character, viewed from the perspective of a critical social theory, is subject to social contingencies that it makes sense to criticize because they can be altered.

The first half of the chapter shows how technology has been implicated by Marxist theorists in all three dimensions of power, as these are defined by Lukes. It begins with a discussion of Marx's indictment of capitalist uses of industrial technology. The first section, "Industrial Capitalism and the Domination of Labour", introduces Marx's argument that capitalist uses of industrial technology negate the essential feature of the human labour process, namely its role as medium of creative self-expression. In capitalist society, technology forces people to do things they would not otherwise have done, rather than enabling them to express themselves better.

This kind of coercion is one-dimensional power, as defined by Lukes. The second section, "Management Science and the Labour Process", introduces twentieth-century labour process theory. According to this perspective, technology designed by capitalism is profoundly inconsistent with the Marxist vision of emancipated labour. At the same time, modern societies exhibit a prevailing consensus that technology is, if not good, inevitable. This consensus is illustrative of two-dimensional power, since it serves some interests more than others and gives rise to symptoms, like the Luddite resistance to industrial looms. In Andrew Feenberg's notion of hegemony within technology design, which is the topic of "Hegemonic Technological Rationality", we find that technology is best understood in terms of three-dimensional power. While it is made up of neutral phys-ical elements, technology enters social activity under descriptions that are inflected by dominant interests. These *codifications* of technology ensure that it seems to be neutral but actually plays a part in the reproduction of social power. The notion of a technological hegemony enables us to re-cast Marx's dialectic in terms of a struggle that takes place within techno-logy design, rather than over its place in social arrangements. The fourth section "Gender and Hegemony" draws on feminist theories of techno-logy to make a critique of Feenberg's notion of a hegemonic technological rationality as the explanatory centrepiece to his theory. I argue that this idea reflects a residual attachment to romantic strains in the substantivist and Marxist traditions that oppose nature to reason. Feminist scholarship high-lights the presence of multiple interests and social logics shaping technology design. The final section "Technology as Discourse" stresses the value of a critical perspective on technology that is tempered by a pragmatic concept of social power rather than informed by post-structuralist thinking on this topic.

Industrial Capitalism and the Domination of Labour

As we saw in the previous chapter, Karl Marx was the first thinker to grasp the society–technology relationship as contradictory. He argued that industrial technology developed under capitalism both enhances human productive capacity and extends the reach of social power so that individuals are increasingly exposed to domination. In the factory system, machinery enhances the productivity of each individual labourer by securing them greater leverage within the production process and enabling them to process raw materials in ever-larger quantities. At the same time the character of this leverage changed. The labour process itself became standardized and uniform, while the social consequence was a loss of distinctions based on skill and craftsmanship. Craftsmen of the era prior to industrialization found that their skills no longer bought them secure employment; they were rendered redundant by innovations like Watt's engine. Craftsmen from weavers through smiths and paper makers all felt the consequences of this technological change. All were reduced to the level of ordinary labourers after having enjoyed higher social status associated with their crafts. In terms of Lukes's three-dimensional theory of power, this change in the form of the labour process shows technology exerting a one-dimensional kind of power. Technology, in this case industrial machines, obliges people to perform actions consistent with its structure. While having to work such a machine in the first place is a result of social factors, the experience of doing it is shaped by the technology. The repetitious and physically demanding experience of nineteenth-century workers was partly a function of machine design.

The contradiction between technology that creates enormous wealth and so should improve everyone's quality of life and the inhumanity that is imposed on most people who have to operate machinery is central to Marx's indictment of capitalism. Technology for Marx points towards a society of material abundance, but also involves more exploitative production relations in which workers' lives are shattered by industrial tools. Technology is fundamental to social domination as well as to progress. Capital develops machinery with the simple aim of producing more goods for less and it uses technology to achieve this by levelling down the skills needed for participation in the labour process and through economies of scale. According to Marx, the driving force here was the desire to extract as much surplus value from workers as possible. Machines were to be used to drive down wages by making all workers replaceable and their efforts correspondingly cheap:

... machinery[1] not only acts as a competitor who gets the better of the workman, and is constantly on the point of making him superfluous. It is also a power inimical to him, and as such capital proclaims it from the roof tops and as such makes use of it. It is the most powerful weapon for repressing strikes, those periodical revolts of the working class against the autocracy of capital...

It would be possible to write quite a history of the inventions, made since 1830, for the sole purpose of supplying capital with weapons against the revolts of the working class.

(Marx 1983: 410–11)

Ironically, through technological development, capitalism creates the possibility of socialism, a society based on material abundance. Industrial machinery will turn out to be beneficial to workers by "quite unintentionally" creating the infrastructure for a new society. Capitalist technology "will redound to the benefit of emancipated labour and is the condition of its emancipation" (Marx 1981: 701).

This implies that, although Marx thought technology was developed by capitalists with exploitation in mind, he held the resulting machines were not themselves tainted by this purpose. In other words, while huge mills with steam-powered looms were destructive to the lives and livelihoods of nineteenth-century weavers, they would serve quite a different function in the future, once the social context had changed. It seems to follow that Marx considered technology was not actually implicated in social power since in itself it brings no problematic social consequences. Changes in the pattern of social organization and not anything inherently retrograde about technology itself lead to regressive uses of technology. In his repudiation of the Luddites and others who would defend the craft element of the labour process against technology, Marx subscribes to the nineteenth-century consensus, discussed in the previous chapter, whereby technology is progress, a view that is not sustainable in its original formulation.

Marx's philosophy puts human creative endeavour at the centre of human affairs, so that under socialism labour is to become "life's prime want", rather than the drudgery that it is under capitalism. This presupposes that labour will change its character under socialism and regain an organic unity within the process of production that it has lost under capitalism. Such a view is implicit when Marx writes of the current marginalization of the worker in the production process:

> Labour no longer appears so much to be included within the production process; rather, the human being comes to relate more as watchman and regulator to the production process itself.
>
> (1981: 705)

Paradoxically, the unity he has in mind seems to resemble that of craft,[2] of the intimate relationship between the artisan, his tools and the raw materials of his trade in a total process of creation that allows the worker to see the creation of each product from start to finish. Marx is both for and against technology, supportive of and opposed to the idea that new technology is progressive. He believed that capitalist industry was a process that had to be endured but that ultimately it would break apart. This would be achieved not through the surface, symptomatic struggles of the Luddites, but because of deeper fissures between the experience of workers on one side and technological advance on the other. Workers' desire to reclaim the integrity of the labour process will be one of the motivating factors for change. This is because labour is more than just means of subsistence; it is also a privileged mode of self-expression and the pivot of collective agency. Attempts to control the labour process through deployment of more technology shatter the craft aesthetic of pre-industrial labour and weaken the power of workers as a class. This aspect of Marx's critique of capitalist technology implies a break with the nineteenth-century consensus and a move towards a deeper, three-dimensional understanding of power in relation to technology. This was developed further by twentieth-century critics of industrial automation.

Management Science and the Labour Process

Capital's attempt to dominate the labour process intensified during the twentieth century. Quantitative analysis of the behaviour of materials, including human materials involved in production, was deployed to subordinate workers and to maximize productivity ratios. In the second half of the century, study of the labour process aimed at further industrial automation reached a new pitch. "Scientific management" involved recording and analyzing the activities of each individual worker throughout the working day. The result was decomposition of the labour process into manageable parts. Sometimes these would even be recorded on film so that a visualization could be used to firm up the definition of each discrete operation. Knowledge of the work process at this level of detail made it possible for management to re-allocate individual tasks to specific workers, intensifying the Fordist system of production line working. Writing in the 1970s, Harry Braverman protested against what he saw as "the reductive formula that expresses both how capital employs labour and what it makes of humanity" (1974: 179). The same attitude, Braverman contends, shapes the design of machines that are used to automate labour processes, once they have been thoroughly described and recorded in detail. In the early 1970s the first cybernetic systems were introduced. These involved robots that simulated human actions on the shop floor and contained feedback control systems so that, as well as being programmed to execute tasks in a specified way, they could also receive data concerning changes in the environment and make changes to performance. These developments, now familiar in all areas of manufacturing in the rich countries of the world, saw the worker moved further to the margins of the productive process.

Braverman associates science and the technical approach with the interests of capital. The key issue here is control over the labour process. Following Marx, Braverman views labour as the fundamental category of human existence (Arthur 2002 and see Rosenthal 1998 for a more critical view). Socialism will transform labour into freely chosen creativity and self-expression. However, what Braverman calls "scientific capitalism" places this, the goal of history, in jeopardy because it chops the labour process into pieces and reduces the labourer to a bit player in the unfolding drama of production. Braverman's account of this is suitably apocalyptic:

> Thus, after a million years of labour, during which humans created not only a complex social culture but in a very real sense created themselves as well, the very cultural-biological trait upon which this entire evolution is founded has been brought, within the last two hundred years, to a crisis, a crisis which Marcuse aptly calls the threat of a "catastrophe of the human essence".
>
> (1974: 171)

The influence of critical theory and its romantic suspicion of science and technology can be seen here in the reference to Marcuse and in the idea that something terrible has happened to the "human essence". It is clear from these comments that Braverman thinks scientific measurement and technology design are biased by their role in these developments. He is explicit in declaring that the result is technology design that embodies the class dynamics of the society that produced it and describes how, as a result of their close working relationship with managers and capital, modern engineers have "internalised" the value of creating machines that facilitate reduced labour costs and made it part of their practice as technologists. This process is so far advanced that reducing costs "appear to them to have the force of natural law or scientific necessity" (1974: 200). Thus capitalism distorts technology development to a point that compromises the neutrality of science and the inherent desirability of technological development.

Braverman's analysis can be read as the application of a three-dimensional theory of power to the capitalist use of technology. In the absence of symptomatic conflict – few people in the 1970s were actually prepared to oppose the introduction of new technology – he argues that the world is being shaped by powerful interests so that such conflict becomes almost impossible. To oppose technology would be against common sense, and yet going along with it is objectively against the interests of most affected parties. When invoking such detrimental consequences for someone's interests under conditions where they themselves do not protest,[3] we stray into the realm of hypothesis. It becomes necessary to show that the interests cited really have been adversely affected and the only way to do this is to describe the situation that would have obtained had power not been present. This involves citing relevant counterfactuals. In his discussion of three-dimensional power Lukes acknowledges that this is a tricky issue. What we have to do is "take steps to find out what it is that people would have done otherwise" (2005: 52), that is, in the absence of social power. In the case of technology this might involve speculating about the likely consequence of a situation without a new technology; the consequences of an alternative technology design that achieves similar purposes but in a different way, or trying to imagine uses of the same technology to achieve different ends, perhaps within an entirely different social context.

David Noble's (1984) study of the automation of the machine tools sector does just this. Machine tools production was one of the last areas of industrial production to be automated, partly because production of these items would be done in smaller quantities than of consumer products. The industry was automated in the 1960s, with the consequence that thousands of skilled jobs were lost forever. Noble shows that when the key decisions in the automation process were taken, engineers and managers had a choice between two automation methods. Both were aimed at expediting the labour process by reducing the amount of effort and therefore the time taken using devices like lathes to produce shaped parts that became components in larger industrial tools. The first was "Record/Playback" (R/P), the second "Numerical Control" (N/C). R/P involved making a literal recording of the actions of a worker as he performed each such task. This recording would then be used to reproduce the motion of the worker automatically – it would be plugged back into the cutting machine, directing its movements in a perfect reproduction of the worker's own actions. N/C in contrast, worked by generating a mathematical model of the worker's actions, a description of each action undertaken by the worker would be constructed in mathematical space. The result was, in effect, a computer programme that could be stored on a card and used whenever needed without subsequent reference to the actions of the worker. The first method retained a role for the worker and, in a sense, the craft element of the process, since the worker could try to perfect the operations needed and choose the best version for automation. The second method was oblivious to these distinctions. Once a programme had been generated that would facilitate creation of a given part it could be attached in a servo-mechanism to the machine formerly operated by the worker and run when necessary. Noble shows that both methods had specific merits and demerits. N/C was seen by some as more elegant but less realistic in the sense that the loss of human attention to detail might be a source of error. In the Soviet Union, R/P methods were preferred for early auto-pilot mechanisms (1984: 85) because they were lighter. R/P, it would appear, was not an objectively inferior method, but it was not selected for use in the machine tools industry. The reasons for this trace to managers' desire to wrest control of the labour process from workers:

> Most importantly, while N/C lent itself to programming in the office, and management control over the process, R/P lent itself to programming on the shop floor, and worker and/or union control of the process.
>
> (1984: 151)

Noble's work is rightly regarded as a seminal text in the sociology of technology and it is an excellent illustration of how the method recommended by Lukes of seeking out implied counterfactuals works to generate critique. He shows that there was nothing inevitable about N/C's victory over R/P; it involved social choices. As he says, "... the point of such an enquiry is not so much to revive a lost alternative as to understand the society that denied it" (1984: 147). The reasons why N/C was preferred had little or nothing to do with efficiency, except on an arbitrarily narrowed definition of that term.

Noble argues that the real explanation was a convergence of interests between the scientists who worked on N/C and managers in the industry, which had been rocked by strikes in the decade prior to automation. He writes that,

> ... the very fact that scientists and engineers are in a position to learn about the properties of matter and energy and to use their knowledge for practical ends, to make decisions about the design and even the use of new technologies, indicates their close relationship to social power.
>
> (1984: 43)

However, it does not follow from this that there is any inherent association between the habits of thinking of engineers and certain kinds of mathematician and the managerial perspective of seeking to gain control over production processes at the expense of labour.[4] Noble overlooks the fact that N/C's mathematical emphasis probably brought other benefits, though these were perhaps obscure at the time, that need to be brought out in a full consideration of the relevant counterfactual. Information on the labour process became portable, for example, in the form of programmes that could move between machines around the world. The information could be acted upon independently of the initial process, so that a whole new level of description and action opens up within the labour process. Designers of new machinery now can programme the whole process of parts construction because it has been modelled to such precision. Machine tools are constructed that generalize the principles of N/C onto a huge scale, including cutting machines that resemble cranes, hundreds of feet tall with workers sitting in cabs mounted high alongside the main machine. At the same time, using mathematical methods the precision of these tools can be calibrated almost indefinitely, to millionths of an inch (Gershenfeld 2005: 76). N/C confers these advantages because it is more abstract and opens up more possibilities within the production process.

The basic principle of N/C underscores technology design in the digital era, where the mobility of informational codes is established as a key feature of economic life. Recent studies of contemporary work highlight the role of ordinary workers using networked computers to process information that is then applied to, largely automated, production and distribution processes.[5] The "knowledge worker" (Kumar 1995) uses the levers provided by this kind of mathematical abstraction to source goods more effectively and tailor production and distribution more flexibly in relation to consumer demand. The contemporary economy has been "informationalised" in this sense (Castells 1996) and this development presupposes the development of tools that quantify over production routines and allow intervention in them by manipulating data structures rather than machines.

I am not suggesting that these possibilities were visible in the 1960s or that they played any explanatory role in the developments described by Braverman and Noble. However, neither author provides a satisfactory account of the social processes whereby methods like N/C get preferred. Instead, they suggest there is an intrinsic association of capitalism and scientific rationality. They do not conceal their distaste for the way that the technological systems aimed at automating production processes they described presupposed detailed studies of human beings. However, measuring the activities of humans as if they were machines is not inherently regrettable or offensive. Management of the labour process becomes regrettable only when it means that people have to do more mindless repetitive tasks for ever-declining amounts of money. Fuller automation, based on accurate measurement of each element of the labour process could, as Andre Gorz (1980) and other advocates of post-industrialism pointed out, free us from the need to work. This vision of a society after capitalism seems more consistent with the technology such a society might actually inherit. The interesting question remains, however: How does social power affect technology design? Braverman and Noble do not tell us what the connection is between the technical reasoning processes that enable us to trace out the inner workings of a machine and the kind of social rationality, against which they both protest, that prioritizes a narrow conception of efficiency (the short-term pursuit of profits) over other social goods associated with technology (like employment). It is implied throughout their analyses that capitalism is inherently related to quantification and to a use of reason that is focused on bringing things under control – nature, people and processes. In other words, it is because capitalism is scientific that technology is implicated in the domination of workers.

Hegemonic Technological Rationality

Andrew Feenberg's critical theory of technology is partly conceived in response to this unsatisfactory situation. Two concepts are particularly relevant here: Dual aspect theory and the theory of formal bias. As we saw in Chapter 2, dual aspect theory is Feenberg's attempt to show that technology can embody valid knowledge and constitute a set of reliable, seemingly neutral tools or points of leverage over nature and *at the same time* constitute an instance of prevailing, hegemonic social rationality and so be implicated in social power. On the one hand, scientific research and the production of useful knowledge that goes into technology design are "to some extent autonomised in the research process" (2002: 78). This process creates elements or parts of technologies that are, in themselves, sociologically unproblematic since they are, at this stage, not used outside of experimental laboratories. It is only when these elements of technology are brought together or "concatenated" in specific designs that technology displays its other aspect. As soon as elements come together in determinate artefacts, the technology begins to take on other meanings that are derived from beyond the research process. It is important to notice that dual aspect theory works well without the potentially confusing idea, discussed in Chapter 3, of primary and secondary instrumentalization. What it says is that any given technology can reasonably be described in terms that specify its workings and the kind of leverage or control it gives us. At the same time, the identical artefact may feature in a description that highlights its efficiency or inefficiency relative to some socially defined purpose. The latter is the function of the technical code under capitalism. The technical code is "the general rule for correlating" the two levels of description, the first of which is purely technical while the second emphasizes efficiency relative to social objectives. When technologies reach the factory or the office they have been "encoded" as efficient tools and, as such, seem unquestionable.

The idea that technology has two aspects, one neutral and technical and the other encoded with social values, enables Feenberg to renew the idea of class antagonism focused on technology, within the tech- nology design process itself. One and the same item of technology can constitute a technical advance by enhancing human capabilities, and have socially regressive consequences. Criticizing technology involves viewing it under both kinds of description and negotiating a course between them, something I have suggested above defines the human relationship to technology. This perspective enables us to shed the idea that techno- logy is substantively biased (as Heidegger would have it) in terms of its cultural consequences, but opens up a more interesting possibility which Feenberg calls formal bias. Substantive bias occurs when a set of rules or a social process specifically favours one group of people over another. An example might be the apartheid system in South Africa, which was instituted through laws that limited the rights of black people and forced them to defer to whites. In contrast, formal bias occurs when a rule that applies equally to everyone systematically results in outcomes deleterious to the interests of one group, even though the rules are formulated in a way that is blind to particular interests. Here the bias is a consequence of the way in which a rule-bound system or device meshes with prior social arrangements. If we view a technical system in abstraction from its social context we will be unable to see its bias, but this is because:

> The bias in such cases originates not in the technical elements but in their specific configurations in a real world of times, places, historical inheritances, in sum, a world of concrete contingencies. The essence of formal bias is the prejudicial choice of the time, place, and manner of the introduction of a system composed of relatively neutral elements.
>
> (Feenberg 2002: 81)

Formal bias is more likely than substantive bias to be a property of tech- nical systems because, as Feenberg points out, "the rationality inherent in technical devices is incommensurable with personal partiality by defin- ition" (2002: 80). So, for example, the assembly line is not a nice place to work but this cannot be traced to any malign properties of the physical elements that constitute it, nor even to their concatenation into a single system, viewed in isolation from its place in the industrial economy.[6] Only when viewed in context can its socially regressive aspect be identified.

A good illustration of formal bias as a critical concept is provided by Goggin and Newell's (2003) *Digital Disability*. They show that the design of digital technologies has effectively precluded the full particip- ation of some groups of people in a society in which economic activity increasingly involves being able to use a computer. The case of blind and partially sighted PC users is particularly interesting here. With the development of the Windows interface as a design standard in the early

1990s, computing became almost overnight a more visual activity. Using a computer efficiently involves clicking on icons, using a mouse to drag and drop items and so on; the grammar of computer use has become centred on the physical manipulation of objects whose presence is mediated by images and icons on a screen. The previous generation of PCs had not been so reliant on visual imagery. Using Braille input devices, blind and visually impaired users had been able to negotiate the command-line interfaces of earlier computers with much greater ease. Windows and a whole generation of software built with Windows in mind meant their expertise with other, less "user friendly" software was no longer valued. There is no suggestion here that the designers of Windows and the other relevant programmes set out to exclude blind users. Indeed, their error and the resulting bias would seem to have been more a consequence of their failure to think about the visually impaired at all. At the same time, computer technology is not inherently visual; this is a matter of design choices. In this sense, then, the technology was not substantively biased. It reflects rather a bias in the technology that stems from a failure to think on the part of technology designers. Here we see the usefulness of Lukes's idea that domination can be the consequence of non-decisions as well as decisions. Formal bias in the concatenation of technical elements results in outcomes that are prejudicial to the interests of groups of people, even though the decisions that led to these design choices were never discussed – they were non-decisions, or the result of common sense in practice.

Feenberg's distinction is intended to take critical theory beyond polarized attitudes towards technology. On one side, Heidegger, green theorists (Eckersley 1990) and eco-feminists (Mellor 1997) seem to think that technology is a substantive evil that must be opposed and criticized. On the other side, Habermas has led the retreat from this to a view of technology as innocent, perhaps even benign when seen in social evolutionary perspective, and beyond critical reproach. Similarly, Donna Haraway and other feminists have rejected the idea that technology is inherently associated with domination. The theory of formal bias allows us to restore technology to the centre of critical theory, while at the same time opening up a margin of manoeuvre for critique that seems to be denied in the more cataclysmic theories described in the previous section. Within this space, Feenberg argues, we find *hegemonic technological rationality*, which orders the integration of technology and social relations under capitalism.

The concept of hegemony was developed by Antonio Gramsci in the 1920s and 1930s. It defines a situation where three-dimensional power has achieved apparent closure so that the organizational form in which it operates allows for no criticism that rejects it as if from outside. Once industrial technology is hegemonic, mounting Luddite style opposition would appear to fly in the face of rationality, hence the term "Luddite" is often unfairly used to suggest people are backward-looking. Gramsci identified common sense, or prevailing popular and practical beliefs, as the typical medium of hegemonic power and argued that, far from being inherently revolutionary, the views of the working class were a kind of eclectic mix of shifting opinions that posed no intrinsic challenge to the status quo (Gramsci 1985: 325, 344; see also Boggs 1976). Industrial technology becomes hegemonic when it is so thoroughly associated with progress and efficiency that rejecting it seems to conflict with this kind of diffuse common sense. Describing this situation as hegemony does not mean conceding that rational criticism is no longer possible. It imposes a strategic re-organization of critique, which now becomes aimed at wresting control over the key terms in the hegemonic ordering itself. Hegemony opens up a new front in social conflicts around technology, wherein there is a "war of position" (Gramsci 1985: 421) in which rather than challenging common sense, different groups deploy their definitions of the ideas of progress and efficiency. Intellectuals have to engage with common-sense ideas and give them a revolutionary impetus or inflection.

Feenberg applies this idea to modern technology. The reason the capitalist technical code works is precisely that technology always appears to be neutral; "common sense" tells us that it is the optimal solution to a given problem and its mere presence in a situation indicates that the problem in question was the most significant one. In this way, technology design is complicit with the pre-structuring of "domain[s] of social activity in accordance with certain interests or values" (2002: 78). The technical code conceals the role of social factors shaping technology design to favour some groups over others behind a veil of technical neutrality. Critical theory of technology appears as a challenge to this hegemonic ordering, which ensures the wholesale acceptance of new technologies as embodiments of the obvious solution to obvious problems. Counter-hegemonic practice consists in showing how seemingly neutral technology has actually been designed so that it benefits some groups at the expense of others. It also includes advocating alternative designs that are technically viable but incorporate broader definitions of what is socially desirable. Counter-hegemony works by re-coding artefacts in such a way as to stretch the limiting effects of the hegemonic technological rationality. Of particular importance here is the idea of efficiency. Efficiency defined in narrow terms is a contingent value, associated with capitalist society and culture rather than integral to technology. But in capitalist societies it seems to be almost the only value that is respected in "good" technology design. This cannot be challenged by calling for less efficient designs, but only by advancing alternative articulations of the technical code. Feenberg (2003) gives the example of boilers on riverboats in the

US, whose boilers were prone to exploding before health and safety legislation was passed in 1852, after a campaign by workers on the boats. In this case, the superior efficiency of steam to other means of propulsion could not be challenged, but the meaning of efficiency was contested and stretched to include appropriate safety standards for workers. This kind of fight for control over the meaning of accepted descriptions is the space within which Feenberg positions a politics of technology.

The idea of a hegemonic technological rationality is intended to encompass what the Frankfurt School called instrumental reason and what Weber analyzed as societal rationalization as these apply to technology design as a social practice. Feenberg introduces it in terms that clearly echo the Frankfurt School's definition of modern instrumental reason:

> An effective hegemony need not be imposed in a continuing struggle between self-conscious agents but one that is reproduced unreflectively by the standard beliefs and practices of the society it dominates. Tradition and religion played that role for millennia; today, forms of rationality supply the hegemonic beliefs and practices.
>
> (2002: 75)

In modern societies being instrumentally rational is common sense and capitalist efficiency is a value that we all strive to maintain. Failure to do so is widely perceived as evidence of some kind of defect, perhaps even immorality. When we ask if our action is sensible or the best course available to us we commonly mean something like "how can I get the most out of this situation for the least amount of effort?" Feenberg argues this form of reasoning is hegemonic in Gramsci's and Lukes's sense. It is present in the background, defining our perceptions and basic categorical ordering of the world and in this way it inclines us towards certain problem definitions and to see some solutions as correspondingly more realistic than others. Yet, although its consequences may be sociologically highly significant, we do not reflect on it and it is rarely questioned. Hegemonic technological rationality enframes the judgements made about technology by key players in the design and implementation process, making some technologies appear sensible and obvious to them while others seem inherently less interesting or likely to succeed. The people making these kinds of choices, like Noble's managers in the machine tools sector, or Braverman's management scientists, operate within a horizon that is set by this hegemonic rationality; they make decisions and judgements, but always within the parameters set by this ordering of the world. When presented with alternative designs they assess them in terms of the hegemonic technological rationality as it applies to their situation. They look for efficiency and they understand this in terms of enhanced control over the production process because this is the way to reduce costs and maximize desired outputs. This, rather than any inherent convergence of interests of scientists and technologists on one side and capitalists and managers on the other, is what ensures that technology serves power. Countering the reductionism in earlier discussions, Feenberg argues that it is the fact that all groups within society work within this artificially narrowed horizon on what counts as good technology that explains why technology often seems to serve power.

However, while the case of visually impaired computer users illustrates formal bias well, it also raises a doubt over whether hegemonic technological rationality in Feenberg's sense is the co-ordinating factor connecting instances where technology seems to be implicated in cases of social injustice or exclusion. At issue there is not rationality but a different kind of limitation on the imaginations of technology designers, one that is perhaps challenged more effectively by a critique of the way that society tends to ignore the needs of disabled people and work within a paradigm of "normality". It is not clear that the kinds of limitation on design targeted by such critique are really captured by the idea of a hegemonic technological rationality. Here designers' failure to think about human diversity seems to be more relevant than an unreflective emphasis on efficiency in the machine. This kind of failure has consequences in many areas of social life and is not specific to technology. As we saw in Chapter 1, this is readily comprehended in Lukes's idea of two-dimensional power – power exerted through decisions that are *not* taken.

Gender and Hegemony

Feminist criticism of technology tends to confirm the idea that while the concept of hegemony and Feenberg's concept of technical politics of design are useful, the notion this hegemony is carried by a particular social rationality is less pertinent. It problematizes the idea that formal bias is the consequence of neutral technical elements concatenated within a horizon set by *capitalist* parsimony while also developing the idea of a social encoding of technology design. In particular, feminism suggests that formal bias occurs when technology designs are shaped by gendered interests as well. In the previous chapter, I argued that technology had been shaped by social logics that worked to the advantage of Europeans, especially property-owning classes, in the modern era. These logics also had a significant gender bias. Feminist explorations of this reveal a logic of masculine pre-eminence within technology design in the modern era.

A pioneering investigation of the shaping of technology in male interests was conducted in the early 1980s by Cynthia Cockburn (2003). Cockburn begins by rejecting biological determinism and essentialism. We have to notice, she says, that gender is a social construct that has effects not only on how we think about ourselves and other people, but also on our bodies and what we make of ourselves physically. Viewed in this way we can see that the relationship between biological sex, physical technology and ideological gender is potentially quite complex. Engaging with technology presupposes a certain physical disposition, which is related to socially constructed ideas about gender. Becoming a person of a specific gender involves using or not using heavy, powerful objects and this means becoming someone with, or lacking specific physical traits. These observations are made by Cockburn in relation to an industrial, male-dominated environment in which being muscular is still very important to holding a dominant position in the workforce:

> ... a small physical *difference* in size, strength and reproductive function is developed into an increasing relative physical advantage to men and vastly multiplied by differential access to technology...
>
> The appropriation of muscle, capability, tools and machinery by men is an important source of women's subordination, indeed it is part of the process by which females are constituted as women.
>
> (Cockburn 2003: 181)

In her study of the print industry, Cockburn highlights that male workers in the industry defended their position of relative advantage within the working class with reference to their skill in manipulating the compositing blocks that made up printed text. This work involved being an adept reader but also considerable physical strength and an appropriate disposition. These factors protected them against capitalist attempts to drive down labour costs (women would be associated with lower wages, see Brenner and Ramas 1984) and enabled them to exclude women from the industry even in the early nineteenth century, when women and children were working in other industrial sectors. Operating the machines was something that most women would not be able to do, due to the heavy physical demands of the work. Here male-dominated trade unions contributed to the shaping of technology to the detriment of women.

In the 1880s, changes in the machinery rendered the argument for female exclusion obsolete. Instead of having to use heavy compositing machinery, linotype and monotype machines made it possible in principle to lay out printing blocks using a keyboard on one machine and another machine for setting or casting. Ultimately, this led to a division of labour within the printing process. Keyboardists would work "upstairs" and their text would then be set as "forme" by men downstairs. The keyboard was identified as a female technology from the 1870s onwards. They had been designed on an analogy with sewing machines – early ones had pedals – and their design emphasized similarities with the piano keyboard, a domestic object. Their introduction coincided with the conversion of the "secretary" from a well-paid male occupation to a low-paid female one (Hartmann 1993). But the forme, which the men worked with, was kept heavy, as were the trolleys and other elements in the workshop. Cockburn argues that this was arbitrary – they could have been smaller and lighter – and reflected the influence of the male workers' ideology. They argued for agreed industrial standards with employers and negotiated on the weight of the equipment to secure their own advantage. Their concern was to emphasize their special skill and their strength, for which they should be paid well. Obviously, it also excluded women, who were seen as neither strong nor intelligent enough to do the work. Cockburn argues:

> ... the appropriation of bodily effectivity on the one hand and the design of machinery and processes on the other have often converged in such a way as to constitute men as capable and women as inadequate. Like other physical differences, gender difference in average bodily strength is not illusory, it is real. It does not necessarily matter, but it can be made to matter. Its manipulation is socio-political power play.
>
> (Cockburn 2003: 190)

Writing in the 1980s, when the old industrial machinery was being replaced by computers, Cockburn notes that the social and political organization of the male print workers will be put to test. In the absence of the arguments and the socially shaped technology, she discusses, their power was of course effectively destroyed by the end of the decade.

Cockburn is not happy with the term "patriarchy" as a way of describing the hegemonic ordering of society, here extended to include the shaping of technology. She argues that this term locates male power too firmly in the family and associates it with fathers. In fact, she suggests, what we have is andrarchy – male power – and this is the hegemonic ideology that is reproduced in technology design. What her study shows is that as far as industrial technology was concerned the machinery was shaped by male interests as well as capitalist ones. In the process, masculinity was itself constructed through a relationship with the technical and this, industrial masculinity, was based on gendered notions of physical strength as well as a capitalist inflection of the ideal of efficiency. This argument is consistent with Feenberg's idea that technology development goes on under a horizon of social values, and Cockburn too foregrounds the construction of the industrial machine as a locus of efficiency and de-aestheticized hardness. At the same time, she maintains that the relationship between gender and technology is one that is constantly open to change and renegotiation. The interesting thing about the introduction of computers from the 1980s onwards, she says, is how male power was re-deployed to produce a new configuration of technology, gender and class identities. These identities are not located in the domestic sphere but precisely in the public encounter with technology. It is interesting to note that, as she anticipated, using a keyboard has lost its feminine connotations with the rise of personal computing and that the computer is unusual in that it is not confined to either the public or private spheres but rather transcends this distinction. Recent feminist scholarship has attempted to update Cockburn's analysis. Judy Wacjman, for example, argues that notwithstanding the move to softer, post-industrial technologies, technology in general remains powerfully shaped by male values and exhibits a formal bias towards the masculine. This makes it off-putting to women because, "men's affinity with technology is integral to the constitution of subject identity for both sexes" (Wacjman 2004: 111). She uses the example of computer culture, where "the masculine workplace culture of passionate virtuosity, typified by hacker-style work, epitomises a world of mastery, individualism and non-sensuality". Consequently, she argues, hegemonic masculinity remains technological and vice versa:

> It is indubitably the case . . . that in contemporary Western society, the hegemonic form of masculinity is still strongly associated with technical prowess and power.
>
> (2004: 112)

However, there is a tension here between Cockburn's argument, which stressed the embodied and physical character of hegemonic masculinity and Wacjman's attempt to re-locate it in technical prowess and subcultures of virtuosity. Indeed, Donna Haraway has argued that the emphasis new technologies place on miniaturization and detail constitute an opening for female participation, since they comport with skills traditionally associated with female gender socialization. She writes that "women's enforced attention to the small takes on quite new dimensions in this world" of computers (Haraway 2000: 295). The gender politics of technology involve renegotiation of the meaning of technology in our idea of the feminine, in light of such changes. In my view it is difficult to make out a credible case for the idea that skill and attention to detail, as distinct from physical strength and disposition, are integral to a masculine gender ideal. Many traditionally female activities like sewing and embroidery involve this kind of skill (see Parker 1986). If hegemonic forms of masculinity are associated with technology then this would make the geek the male ideal.[7] Hegemonic technological rationality seems to be becoming somewhat of a stretched notion, a theme I will rejoin in Chapter 7. It now includes ideas about the normal physical human subject, notions about gender and identity *and* is at the same time associated with a reduction of investments of meaning in technology associated with capitalist de-aestheticization.

Technology as Discourse

Feenberg aims to accommodate these tensions within the idea of a hegemonic technological rationality by embracing post-structuralist theories that have been used to develop Gramsci's idea of hegemony.[8] According to this perspective, the idea that technology design is constrained by deeply ingrained and hard to challenge ideas about what counts as technology can be likened to the hold of other historically contingent ideas concerning what is normal in human affairs. Sociologically neutral discoveries are combined in ways that mirror the post-structuralist notion of discourse. Feenberg draws the analogy between technology design and the discursive constitution of social reality in the following terms:

> I will reserve the term "technical element" for the specific principles, such as the spring, the lever or the electric circuit. These are in themselves "relatively" neutral, if not with respect to all social purposes, at least with respect to the ends of ruling and subordinate social groups. The work of discovering such elements is to some extent autonomised in the research process. Once discovered, they are like the vocabulary of a language; they can be strung together – encoded – to form a variety of "sentences" with different meanings and intentions.
>
> (2002: 78)

This comment is reminiscent of the argument advanced earlier that technology merits consideration as a kind of universal language spoken by human beings through their actions on and through the propensities of things. The way they present to us, the possibilities artefacts afford us and what they are like to use are all matters of interpretation.[9]

However, Feenberg pursues the analogy with language not to re-situate technology as a field of repeated statements within the context of a theory of its meaning-interpretation, but instead to align it with a

Foucauldian idea of discourse. According to Foucault, truth itself is an effect of power (Foucault 1980: 131). Some discourses are invested with truth and this means that they have a dual relationship with power. On one side, they are called upon to produce truth in accordance with the stipulations of power, on the other they constitute power in practice as they incorporate human individuals and produce them in accordance with the truth as prescription. In his studies of madness and the clinic, for example, Foucault uncovers the production and effectiveness of truth in the context of the discursive regimes of psychiatry and medicine (Foucault 1985, 1986). The idea of madness was produced as a truth concerning certain forms of human behaviour and constituted a crucial delineation of human subjects in the modern period. Once the idea that some people were abnormal or insane became instituted in the discourse of psychiatry, it was necessary to have this distinction policed by experts who could recognize the signs of mental disturbance. Doctors and psychiatrists became conduits for the mixture of truth and power that is psychiatric discourse, channelling and processing their patients through treatments and cures deemed appropriate by the new discourse. Those classed as mad experienced the power of the new discursive regime in the form of various kinds of imprisonment and the application of techniques aimed at getting them to recognize the truth of the delineation.[10] Acceptance of this truth is not merely a cognitive operation but a process whereby the subject internalizes the perspective of the reigning discourse on their own behaviour. The turning point in any such treatment comes when the patient is able to tell when their behaviour is "normal" and when it is not. At this point, the discourse begins to produce them as normalized subjects and they are effects of its combination of truth and power.

Foucault's analysis of the power/knowledge relation has been highly influential on attempts to develop and apply Gramsci's idea of hegemony. Post-structuralism purports to reveal concentrations of power within everyday mechanisms of linguistic communication. Personal identity is itself viewed as an effect of this kind of power, so that individual agents are constructed by being hailed, or interpellated, by discourses. The distinction between subject and object falls away as individual identities are read as effects of discourse and associated practices. A person described as "mad" is constructed through interpellation by psychiatric discourse and clinical practice. These processes produce their behaviour and its categorization. The science that discloses facts about the physical brain states of such patients is, from this perspective, also implicated as a component part of the discursive regime, rather than a privileged perspective on it. The intentions of this approach can be emancipatory, because they open up room for manoeuvre within hegemonic discourses like those produced around mental illness. Through patient groups and political movements, like the Anti-psychiatry movement, people can respond to a given discursive regime, making strategic re-deployments aimed at re-defining truth for a certain class of actions, events and subjects. The classic illustration of such a counter-hegemonic struggle was the successful effort to prise same-sex desire out of the discourse of psychiatry, where it was classed as a disease, and into a positive, celebratory discourse and cultural practices that invoked a "new" truth, namely the naturalness and morality of homosexual desire. Feenberg's theory of technical politics is an attempt to politicize technology design[11] through a similar strategy.

Technological hegemony, he says, works because technical reason and its imperatives are "encoded" in technological artefacts. What they "say", then, becomes both an expression of knowledge (it speaks of the afford-ances it opens up and it does this by being a manipulation of the relevant elements in the world) and of power (it is a solution to this problem rather than that one and it solves it in this way rather than that). Rather than coming at a technology and trying to work out how to use it, the human subject is in a sense constituted by the object; produced as a user as an effect of its power. Using technology still involves experimenting with different moves and assessing the artefact's response to see if they are appropriate but in Foucauldian terms this is exploring the margin of manoeuvre allowed us by disciplinary power. Aligning technology with discourse in this way enables Feenberg to view the hegemonic codifica-tion of technical elements that defines capitalist technology as a kind of contestable "truth". Once the contested character of "normal technology" is exposed its users can extend the cultural horizon that limits "what counts" as valid technology to include those technological statements, or designs, that comport with their ideas of what technology is and what it should be for. Such progressive interventions within technology design and use are called "progressive" or "democratic rationalisations", since they articulate the instrumentalizing power of technology to emancip-atory ends through a re-articulation of the technical code. The notion that there is one optimal design, or of "correct" use, is seen here as an effect of power that needs to be overturned. A similar alliance with post-structuralism can be found in much recent feminist writing, a theme I will resume in the next chapter.

However, Feenberg's development of the idea of technological hegemony must be set within certain limiting conditions or para-meters that apply to any sociologically motivated critique of truth. Here, Lukes's (2005) critique of Foucault applies to Feenberg's critical theory of technology. Lukes's argument has three aspects relevant to assessment of Feenberg's theory. The first concerns the criteria we employ for saying that an exercise of power matters and the relationship between this claim and our normative ideas about power and domination. The second concerns our ability to make a critique of power, in the absence of reliable standards of truth that can be applied to the situation we are assessing. Finally, there is a problem elaborating the normative bases of the Foucaultian critique of power as domination, resulting from Foucault's collapsing of all normative discourses into the same historical mass where he locates those invidious disciplinary discourses that are his targets. Each line of criticism has implications for the critical theory of technology.

Power only matters when it results in outcomes that someone somewhere has cause to regret. Overlooking this and delving into what Foucault calls the "micro-politics" of power threatens endless analyses targeting power that does not really matter.[12] The point here is that such power is not really power at all, recalling that, for Lukes, power is an inherently normative concept that we invoke when we are concerned that a situation or event is being shaped unfairly to the disadvantage of a person or group. To speak of power is to invoke some standard of relevance that, while it may not be visible immediately to all who encounter your argument, should emerge in the course of discussion and be capable of producing an appropriate sentiment of regret in any reasonable audience. Applied to technology, we can see that Noble's and Cockburn's studies have this intention. However, we can also envisage instances of sociologically unproblematic technologies. This is easily done in the case of small appliances like pencils, toothbrushes or cutlery. These items unproblematically ease our lives in accordance with the anthropological–instrumental definition of technology discussed in Chapter 2. Critical theory's attitude towards technology barely allows the possibility of such items, whose codification seems far removed from any "capitalist logic" and whose associated customs and logic of use are deeply ingrained in cultural practices that are not worth criticizing. Clearly, technology is always socially constructed but at any given point in history there are whole layers of it that we do not seek to criticize and transform, but learn about and trust. Not all technology is appropriate subject matter for critique.

The second point is related to this one and it concerns how we are to make relevant criticisms and how we should assess other people's criticisms of technology design as a manifestation of social power. Foucault's idea of a regime of truth posits a striking association of rationality and power, but if rationality really is shot through with power as he suggests then we lack an Archimedean point from which to lever a critique. Citing Spinoza, Lukes argues that it is natural to oppose reason and freedom to power: "Power is present where the body is constrained or the mind cannot reason to its own conclusion" (2005: 87). The significance of these observations is that they provide us with an understanding of hegemonic power – it is present when people behave in a way that runs counter to their own interests because they have insufficient information about the viable alternatives, or these alternatives have been discredited in advance by unfair means. In such cases, we can argue that people have not been able to exercise their own reason to determine their best course of action. This is a denial of their basic autonomy. To demonstrate the presence of such, by definition unseen constraints, we can deploy the method of the counterfactual, discussed above. This involves hypothesizing that rather than pursuing the course they did, agents might instead have done something else and then speculating as to the likely outcomes of such an eventuality (Hawthorn 1995). In this way, we can envisage an alternative universe and assess whether the agents' interests might have been better served there. If a good argument can be made for saying this, then there seems to have been a failure of rationality on the part of our actors and the exercise of power, in the form of some tangible constraint, can be cited as part of the explanation.

This approach does not invoke power as a separate substance in the world, as some critics of critical theory have suggested (Latour 2005), but as a normative category that points up the possibility and desirability of doing things differently in future. It requires a theory of the human being as a rational creature that wants to live and uses reason to work out how best to conduct itself from day to day – a being that wants to learn. The problem is that if we concede to Foucault the idea that the human desire to learn is in itself merely an effect of power – to be instilled through application of disciplinary mechanisms and a discourse that separates the normal from the pathological – then we cannot make sense of the implied counterfactual. There would then be no reason for people to prefer non-exploding boilers that was not itself an effect of power. Applied to technology in the broadest sense, we must conclude that all people have a rational interest in safe, reliable and life-enhancing technology. There are (quasi-)universal principles that underscore good technology design and part of the task of critical theory of technology must be to elaborate these.

The final point concerns the normative basis upon which critique of technology as serving social power is made. Following Lukes, I have argued that this requires the method of the counterfactual applied carefully to specific instances of technology design. This kind of critique presupposes a conception of what human beings are like, namely that we are rational and that we seek to use our own reason to work out what course we want to follow. Applied to technology, it also assumes that artefacts have a kind of coherence that enables us to incorporate them into our action repertoires in a way that is not harmful to us and that they help us to achieve ends that are consistent with generalizable human interests or values we may plausibly conceive that any rational person would be able to identify with. This, Habermasian formulation applies to ethical critique in general and works here as a pragmatic perspective from which we can criticize particular technology designs. Like Marcuse, Feenberg argues that when we criticize contemporary technology we invoke the possibility of an entirely different configuration of society and technology, which he calls an alternative "civilizational model". I think this is over-ambitious but also unnecessary. Such broad concepts are irrelevant to reforms of the kind Feenberg advocates to the design process, which are aimed at making it more participatory and democratic. Whereas for Foucault there is no truth independent of the operations of power, it is clear that in reality technological capabilities do have better and worse possible realizations and that these exist as implied counterfactuals that can be deduced from the design process.

The Limits of Social Constructionism

5

We take a social constructionist attitude towards something when we believe that its appearance of permanence, naturalness or solidity is actually contingent upon the actions of human individuals in society. This perspective is particularly surprising when applied to institutions and practices that have been reified (Berger and Luckmann 1976), so that they seem to be constants of human existence, beyond the reach of reform through intentional human action. Some authors within the philosophy of science (Bloor 1976 and in a somewhat different way Kuhn 1970) argue that nature, biology and matter are themselves social constructs in this sense. The argument is that rather than reflecting necessary interpretations of recalcitrant and incorrigible features of the world, these categories are human productions, created and sustained by people whose primary influences and constraints are social in origin. For constructionism, science and technology are socially produced and their guiding principles best understood in this light.

This chapter begins by presenting a constructionist account of the contemporary personal computer. The discussion is aimed at highlighting the open character of digital technology to being shaped by social forces. At the same time, it emphasizes that when technology limits or determines human action this is not always a matter of the artefact imposing a technical order, or instrumental reason on human activities. Technology does always do this to some extent, but social power may be channelled through technology designs that do not emphasize instrumentalism or even, as in the case of contemporary computer designs, actually inhibit it. The second section "Cyborgs and Post-humans" then examines some attempts to comprehend computer and digital technology from a feminist standpoint, deepening the discussion opened up in the previous chapter. It has been argued that the openness of digital communications networks effects such drastic changes that it necessitates a fundamental revision of our conceptual or categorical framework for social analysis. Donna Haraway, for example, argues that we are all now "cyborgs"; fusions or assemblages of humanity and machinery. In a similar vein, N. Katherine Hayles has suggested that our new dependence on digital technologies and others in which codification seems to be more important than material substance shifts us to a situation that she calls "post-human". For both authors, the changes involved present us with a changed methodological scenario for the human sciences and for social and cultural analysis. This theme is taken up in the third section "The Agency of Things" which discusses the recent work of Bruno Latour who also believes that the distinction, until now fundamental to sociology and the other humanities disciplines, between humans and machines has been superseded by contemporary technological and social developments. He recommends that sociology looks again to see what is actually there in what we are habituated to thinking of as the "social". In his opinion, what we see are not societies at all, in the substantive and normative sense of that term as it is used in traditional sociology, but assemblages and networks of people and objects. Rather than assuming that human/object is the key distinction to be drawn, he argues we should study the dynamics of these assemblages and networks and reach conclusions as to where the most important distinctions are to be drawn *after* we have done this work.

In the concluding section "The Limits of Constructionism", I argue that while constructionism's central insight must be retained, any viable theory of technology needs to balance the role of proximal social and cultural determinants that shape technology design against that of anthropologically given interests. The physical character of technology, which warrants a kind of priority to scientific disciplines, also should not be overlooked. Similarly, the normative dimension of social theory involves commitment to the privileged status of the human creature as both inherently rational and as wanting to be free. How these properties become articulated to questions of social structure and technology design varies historically, but they are essential to any understanding of technology and its relation to social power.

Constructionism and Digital Technology

As seen in Chapter 2, Bijker's notion of the semiotics of technology is intended to grasp the role of power in the reification of technical designs. He argues that through interaction with people technologies become objects with determinate meanings. In this process, which is an instance of the "micro-politics of power" (1997: 236), they take on a kind of fixity or solidity:

> To the extent that meanings become fixed or reified in certain forms, which then articulate particular facts, artefacts, agents, practices, and relations, this fixity is power. Power thus is the apparent order of taken-for-granted categories of existence, as they are fixed and represented in technological frames.
>
> (1997: 263)

In this way, technology is aligned with structural social power and works in a similar way to social institutions that reify certain practices by making them seem natural and obvious.[1] At the same time, this power is productive for individuals encountering technology. Bijker emphasizes that interacting with technology and accepting its authority, so to speak, also enables us to explore its possibilities. In this sense, technology use involves what he calls a "micro-politics". What he calls the technological frame, "also enables its members by providing problem-solving strategies, theories, and testing practices, for example, which form the micro-political aspect of power" (1997: 264). He aligns this idea of power as both prescriptive and productive with Foucault's notion of disciplinary power. Like Feenberg, he encourages us to view technology as a mode of discourse, which constitutes the subject and its capacities while at the same time inserting an inescapable social logic into its procedures. Just as subjectivity includes a "margin of maneouvre" that is fraught with risks – being labelled as deviant, ill, criminal or insane – so technology includes similar scope for legitimate experimentation within the confines of the technological frame. As with Foucault's conception, Bijker argues that this conception of power is analytical rather than normative, it is "morally neutral" (1997: 262).

However, it makes little sense to use power in a non-evaluative sense because the term always carries the implication that things would be different in its absence and that they would be so in a way that might matter. This is not to deny that technology is associated with the kind of fixity or seeming solidity Bijker refers to, nor that this is often problematic. It is to suggest that these things do not always go together and that it is worth developing a critical theory of technology and its relation to social power that is capable of singling out developments that reflect the operation of power and are, in fact, of real significance. A surer way of handling the concept would be to recognize its inherently normative character, as was argued in the previous chapter. This requires that we afford privileged status to the technical standpoint, from which we can establish what the available possibilities are in relation to a technology at any given time. For Bijker, the technical standpoint enjoys pre-eminence in experience only because it is backed up by social power. However, this conflates the real constraints that come with a technology with those that are "designed-in". The history of the personal computer problematises the inherent association of technical reason with social power and suggests that the frame that limits our experience need not be peculiarly "technological", in the sense of being opposed to communicative or aesthetic dimensions of experience. Moreover, technical knowledge may be a stake in "micro-politics", so that expertise cannot be viewed merely as a social effect. The technical standpoint does not determine, but it does constrain the available alternatives. The non-technical perspective supervenes on the technical one in the sense described in Chapter 2, and it is here that social interests enter the scene of technology design.

The constructionist ideas of "relevant social group", "interpretative flexibility" and "stabilisation" introduced in Chapter 2 can be illustrated with reference to the history of the personal computer (PC), which has its origins in the small, home- or micro-computers of the 1970s and 1980s. The first such machine was the Altair 8800, which was sold through an advert in the American "Popular Electronics" magazine in 1974 (Ceruzzi 2000: 225). These computers were sold by mail order in the form of kits containing parts that had to be put together by the purchaser. A lights display on the front of the case seems to have been the only output device, while "commands" were entered by flicking switches, also on the front of the machine. Most Altairs were never successfully constructed (Freiberger and Swaine 1984; Levy 1984) and the ones that were acquired their function or purpose from the technical enthusiasts who made them. In Feenberg's phrase, home computers were launched onto the market with "infinite promise and few applications" (1999: 85). During the 1980s, home computers came with screens and keyboards, but tiny memories and processors. These machines include the Commodore, the biggest selling computer of this time. Many such machines were produced in different countries around the developed world with no real attempt to standardize their design and conflicting ideas circulating about their purposes. The large companies that had been involved in manufacturing computers for the military, other branches of government and larger private organizations were not interested in this market throughout the 1970s and 1980s. IBM in particular, whose processors were used in other firm's microcomputers, showed no interest in making small machines for home use, apparently believing that this would always be a small, niche market. In the UK alone several small machines were produced, including the Dragon computer and the Acorn as well as the BBC micro. In other European countries there were also attempts to manufacture micro-computers, including Eastern Europe, which was then within the Soviet sphere of influence.[2]

Discrete constituencies formed quite quickly around the new devices, mirroring the diverse social responses to the bicycle mentioned previously. Computer hackers, for example, focused on the hardware level of the machine and tended to experiment with what it could do. They were more interested in testing the limits of the computer as a complex calculator and in getting it to do new tricks than in using software that was bought "off the shelf" to run on home computers. Hackers were part of the 1960s' hippy counterculture (Roszack 1968) and many of them associated computers with a potential for increased democracy (Levy 1984; Markoff 2006). Another important constituency of this period was the burgeoning computer game sector. The most successful micro-computers of the 1980s, in the US and Europe, were Commodore and Spectrum machines. These were initially presented to the public as business tools for small enterprises. The idea expressed in this publicity was that just as large corporations could use computers to process payroll and other functions involving large batches of data, so smaller businesses could save time by using micro-computers for similar kinds of process. However, these machines were famously appropriated by "bedroom coders" (Newman 2004); young people who made and distributed their own computer games for use within their peer group. Games would be swapped on cassette tapes, in the case of Spectrum games, or on floppy discs. Sometimes code for games would be printed in enthusiast magazines and people would copy it into their machines in order to play the games, or floppies would be attached to the magazines as free offers. In communist-run Poland, there was even a radio station that broadcast programmes for the Spectrum, which users would record using radios and cassette players, and then run on their computers (Kirkpatrick 2007).

The interpretations each group had of the computer at this time certainly had consequences for subsequent designs. As it became apparent that the Spectrum was being defined as a gaming machine, for example, the company that made them focused more on keeping the machines cheap and emphasizing their "futuristic" appearance. This meant that they had less memory capacity than rival machines and than was technically feasible for a machine the size of the Spectrum at that time.[3] The absence of standard memory storage protocols at this stage meant that programmes for one machine could not be made to work on others. For some machines, especially the Commodores and Spectrums, there were many game programmes and ingenious means developed of circulating these within the gaming peer group. Once this dynamic was set in motion, Spectrums and Commodores gained in popularity while others competed for the market in business uses. Other computers, such as the BBC micro or the Polish Meritum seem to have been perceived by everyone primarily as educational devices and so fewer games were produced for them (see Selwyn 2002, 2003). Educational software producers in the UK tended to make programmes that would run on the BBC Micro. Business applications were written for nearly all the machines, with varying levels of success. Although some machines were favoured by certain constituencies the fit was not a tight one – Spectrums were used in university laboratories, for example, and people played games on their BBC machines.

The IBM-PC, which was launched in the US in 1986, was widely seen as the first "professional" computer and with its relatively large memory and unprecedented processing speeds it soon became the machine of choice for users of all orientations. The early period of diversity and experimentation in PC hardware gave way to one of stability and closure. However, the main socially driven changes in computer design centred not on the hardware but on the software and the machine interface. Characteristic of all the machines just discussed and the PC itself was an austere interface based on command lines. Commodores and early PCs alike confronted their users with a blank screen containing some minimal text and a cursor. To access any functions users had to know some of the commands that would enable them to send instructions to the machine through its operating system. Without knowledge of the operating system's syntax it would be impossible to make it do anything; even running a game programme required users to know the term for "run a program" and normally the "address" of the programme, by which the processor could identify its location and begin the process. This austere interface was intellectually taxing and in this sense, these were closed machines that excluded non-expert people from being able to use them, even to play games. Viewed in another way, however, computers before the advent of Windows and its "easy to use" syntax of pointing, clicking and navigating were actually more open. For hackers and hobbyists who enjoyed probing the depths of the machine or testing out its physical limitations, the new interfaces presented an obstacle. The computer was being "black-boxed" and its innards concealed from view.

This development saw the emergence of a new sub-discipline within computer science, "human–computer interaction" (H–CI). H–CI is the study of interface design and it includes the disciplinary norm that computers should be tools with which people achieve things, rather than objects of fascination in themselves. As Sherry Turkle pointed out at the time:

> Professional computer scientists work to develop technology that does not demand technical knowledge of its users to develop "human interfaces" that will make relating to computers more like holding a conversation and less like taking apart a bicycle.
>
> (1984: 194)

The computer interface is there to relieve the user of cognitive burdens associated with using the machine.[4] H–CI specialists became a visionary group within the computer industry from the early 1990s onwards. From this point on there were two socially relevant groups actively involved in the design of the PC: The technicians and programmers who had always been involved in designing electronic systems and the interface designers who held out a vision of non-technical computing. Technicians tended to view interface design as a "soft" pursuit that lacked the demanding character of their work with computers. There is evidence that they resented the appropriation of computers by "human factors" specialists. Nicholas Negroponte (1995), for example, recalls being derided as a "cissy" for his interest in creating intelligent and flexible interfaces that would enable computers to disappear into the users' environment. Similar comments can be found elsewhere in the interface design literature (see Laurel 1993: 48; Johnson 1997: 58). Interface designers for their part viewed technicians as a "priesthood" who wanted to keep computers mysterious in order to preserve their own status. The conflict between technicians and interface designers had a clear winner in the sense that no one now buys a new PC with an austere, command-line interface. This victory coincided with the adoption and further shaping of computers by powerful forces within the modern economy. As Castells (1996) and others have shown, the information processing power of digital computers has become fundamental to modern commerce. It is as a user-friendly tool rather than an object of intrinsic fascination that the computer has reconfigured modern capitalist economies. In this form it has become reified, so that we encounter the PC with a specific set of expectations, taking for granted that our repertoire of pointing and clicking will enable it to work; that its screen and speakers will tell us everything we need to know to have a smooth uninterrupted experience, and that we will be guided by the machine to completion of our objective. These expectations in a sense define what the PC has become – its reified form – so that we forget that each item on the list was the outcome of a choice and that other possibilities were neglected in that process.

We can see from this that it is an error to conflate the element of social power in design with that of technical reason or instrumental action. Failing to distinguish them leads Bijker to identify the power of technology with the imposition of a technical rationality on people through the agency of things. Like Feenberg, he neglects the possibility that technology design can also be implicated in power by being aimed at impeding and curtailing users' technical understanding. In this way, power distorts the translation process between the two sides of the technological frame, ensuring that while engineers see one thing, users may be encouraged to see and learn something altogether less interesting but more in keeping with what their employers, or the government, want them to see.

Cyborgs and Post-humans

For many feminist scholars, digital technology constitutes an opening in the history of technology. There are at least three reasons for this. First, digital technology is informational. It provides instrumental leverage over information, rather than over elements in the natural world. It is economically useful because the enhancement of information processing power facilitates improvements in the traditionally more central dimensions of economic activity, production and distribution. The fact that it works at a kind of distance from these, traditionally male-dominated spheres, however, means that productive technology may be shorn of the masculine bias which, as we saw in the previous chapter, it acquired in the industrial era. Secondly, digital technology has not been limited in its application to the economic sphere. Unlike other productive technologies, it has entered the domestic and cultural spaces and practices traditionally occupied by women. The fact that the first small computers came to be known as "home" computers is indicative of this, as indeed is their subsequent designation as "Personal". PCs have become important communications tools, extending to the recent development of "community" websites like "MySpace" and "FaceBook". Computer technology here seems to be shaped by feminine interests and to be the locus of expressive and creative activities that are not overtly gendered. Viewed in this way it constitutes an opportunity for a feminist technical politics. This departs radically with eco-feminist positions, for which technology is essentially masculine and opposed to a feminine nature. The computer here responds to a desire expressed by other feminists to escape the limits of "natural" embodiment and move towards a use of technology as a resource with which to overcome gender inequality.[5] Thirdly, for some thinkers, especially Donna Haraway and N. Katherine Hayles, the development of computers involves a new historical situation in which not only gender differences but also traditional distinctions like those between the human and the inorganic seem to lose their hold. There is an opening here for a practical reconfiguration of gender, nature and technology. In Haraway's (1997) thinking, contemporary "technoscience" necessitates a re-working of our most basic categorical schema for ordering the world.

In N. Katherine Hayles's (1999) work, digital technologies are implicated in a cultural shift that she calls the move to "post-humanism". This shift involves the emergence of a culture of virtuality around the computer.

Where other theorists have tended to take this idea for granted as an effect of the representational power of computers, in particular their capacity to generate perceptually compelling "worlds" of experience that have no real world referent, Hayles shows how virtuality is the effect of social investments that have shaped the computer over the past three decades. The idea of the virtual originates in a culturally diffuse sense that codes and patterns are more important determinants of the character and content of experience than material substances. This sense can be traced to the discovery of DNA in biology in the 1950s as well as to the significance of mathematically ordered programmes that control the behaviour of computers. In both cases what we find is that mobile and fluid codes determine our experience. The physical elements of organic bodies are constant to all members of our species, but our individual differences stem from a code that we cannot see. Similarly, computers are indeterminate ugly boxes until different programmes, whose code we do not examine, transform them into the loci of a seemingly endless list of operations and practices, from word processing to slaying fictional aliens. Hayles emphasizes that, in a sense, this perception of the relative importance of mobile and intangible codes is ideological, after all " ... for information to exist, it must always be instantiated in a medium" (1999: 12). Notwithstanding this, once it takes a hold the culture of virtuality succeeds in shaping computer technology, so that it effectively becomes a series of "virtual machines". In this way, Hayles writes, "the perception of virtuality facilitates the development of virtual technologies, and the technologies reinforce the perception" (1999: 14).

The computers we end up with, however, are not "ideological" machines. Through them the idea of virtuality becomes concrete. In Hayles's terms there is a kind of dialectic between the ideology and its material realization in technology designs. This involves a movement between, on one side, the incorporation of computer technologies into a physical repertoire of actions on the part of human beings and, on the other, new kinds of cultural self-reflection in response to these changes. What Sean Cubitt (2000) calls the "physical grammar" of contemporary computing, with its "cutting and pasting", "dragging and dropping" and so on, Hayles comprehends as the physical *incorporation* of the technology into our lives. Through incorporation, computer technology becomes part of an embodiment relation, essential to a historically and culturally specific physical mode of experiencing the world. At the same time, this process is itself reflected upon and written about, which gives us a discursive representation of the technology and its significance, which can also affect subsequent designs. Hayles calls this the "inscription" of the technology. One effect of this dialectic is to open up a discrepancy between the experience of incorporation and embodiment on one hand

and the meaning we attach to our own activities, including our bodies, on the other:

> ... when people begin using their bodies in significantly different ways, either because of technological innovations or other cultural shifts, changing experiences of embodiment bubble up into language, affecting the metaphoric networks at play within the culture. At the same time, discursive constructions affect how bodies move through space and time, influence what technologies are developed and help to situate the interface between bodies and technologies.
>
> (1999: 207)

In this way, a tension is produced between embodiment as practical processes of incorporation and the body as an object in critical discourse and as a vehicle for ideas about self-hood and identity. This is a similar distinction to the one discussed earlier between technology as learned and habitual on one side and its capacity to take on meanings that may be renegotiated on the other. As we have seen, both aspects are present in any experience of technology. Hayles's thesis relocates these levels of description in a theory of the body. She identifies the possibility of discrepancies between embodiment experienced through the incorporation of technology and our discursively mediated sense of our bodies as our "selves".

This discrepancy forms the basis, for Hayles, of a kind of technical politics that would take as its goal some mediation of embodiment and the body. The virtual nature of modern technologies makes it possible to launch interventions in the inscription of technology, motivated by a progressive interest in greater freedom. At the same time, Hayles refuses the idea that the body is a natural entity, which would enable her to side with feminists for whom there is an intrinsically superior way of relating to nature that is uniquely feminine, or indeed to align her critique with romantic strains of critical theory. Instead, she insists that discursive interventions in "post-human" politics are guided by situation-specific imperatives arising out of the culture of virtuality itself. There is no intrinsically desirable human project determined by properties of the human creature. Contemporary society is post-human in the sense that there is no "natural" human good towards which we should aspire. The meaning of freedom, for instance, is always partly contingent on other kinds of technological enhancement that define current embodiment relations. The stable "self", essential to traditional theories of autonomy, is not necessary to Hayles's "situated" concept of freedom. She writes that "a coherent, continuous, essential self is neither necessary nor sufficient to explain embodied experience" (1999: 201).

A similar approach to the social construction of digital technology is taken by Donna Haraway. Haraway is suspicious of the notion of virtuality (cited in Shields 2003: 4), but both thinkers share a vision in which the human subject as privileged locus of intentionality has been displaced and dispersed by the development of "intelligent" or behaviourally complex networks.[6] In Haraway's terminology these networks combine the actions of individuals with machine behaviour to produce novel combinations or cyborgs. Technoscience, including nuclear and bio-technologies, have "changed who we are fundamentally and permanently (1997: 56)". Cyborg assemblages are salient formations from the standpoint of a social analysis that has given up the prejudicial privileging of the human individual. Humans are merged with machines in novel hybrids and the beings we are used to thinking of as individual humans are also dispersed across more than one such entity. The idea of a sovereign self presiding over the different combinations in which any given biological individual may be involved is, for Haraway, inherently suspect. Moreover, the human element in these cyborgs necessitates no distinctive methodological response since, "human beings, like any other component or sub-system, must be localised in a system architecture whose basic modes of operation are probabilistic, statistical" (Haraway 2000: 302). The rules of behaviour of post-human, cyborg entities are disclosed by communications engineering (2000: 301), rather than hermeneutics or interpretation. Since social relations now consist in codified information passing between bio-machines, there is no "human" point from which to work in developing a critique. Haraway asserts, however, that while this scenario involves a new kind of power, which she calls "the informatics of domination", it also opens up the possibility of resistance in the form of "theories of the text" (2000: 301) or "cyborg semiologies", which focus on the coded character of this new world situation and allow cyborgs to create "political-fictions", of which the cyborg itself is an example, that introduce perturbations into the system. This notion, of a meaningful alternative to the all-encompassing bio-technical system launched from within is similar to Feenberg's idea of a technical politics, in the sense that it emphasizes ambivalence in contemporary rationalization processes, where these are linked to technology development. This ambivalence extends to the idea that the system has two aspects – one grasped by communications science, the other by cyborg semiotics – and, also like Feenberg, she contrasts the meaning-orientation of the latter with the technocratic character of the former (for Haraway, language is actually opposed to communication in the sense that meaning outflanks and blocks the merely mechanical exchange of information). However, developing her rhetorical notion of "technoscience" she implies that these analytical distinctions can no longer be drawn, since "the technical,

textual, organic, historical, formal, mythic, economic and political dimensions of entities, actions and worlds implode in the gravity well of technoscience" (1997: 68). Hayles and Haraway, then, break the association
of technology's reification and its service to power with instrumentalism
as a modality of action, but in so doing they make the idea of a human
individual into a contingent social construct. On this basis, Haraway
finds the new cyborg scenario is an opportunity for progressive political
action. Women in particular, she argues, can cast aside the construction of
traditional female identity, including eco-feminist myths concerning the
positive value of specifically female, "natural" embodiment. The new situation presents previously unthought of possibilities for experimentation.

However, there are a number of problems with the "post-human",
cyborg positions elaborated by Hayles and Haraway. In particular, the
hold of invariant constraints arising out of biology and anthropology
on technology design limits the plausibility of their thesis. The diffusion
of electronic networks transmitting information requires material interfaces with human users for its operation. These interfaces are designed
specifically to be used by human individuals with determinate cognitive
capacities. They are the points at which human beings gain access to
information and affect its flows. While Hayles and Haraway acknowledge
that there is a politics concerning the process whereby the human (as
fragmented intentional agent, but also as a hybridized organic entity)
bonds with the machine, they do not recognize important continuities
on the human side of this relationship. Generalizing from aspects of the
human encounter with contemporary technologies, they efface persistent
features of the technological and the human that are not "reconfigured"
and actually limit the scope of the cyborg or post-human scenario.

This can be illustrated by the case of "rape in cyber-space", reported by
Julian Dibbell (1993) and discussed by Turkle (1995). This event took place
in the on-line, text-based "world", LambdaMOO, which was one of the
first multi-player games.[7] "Cyber-rape" occurred when one player was able
to use their programming skills to take control of another player's character and make it appear as if she participated in sexual acts with them, in
the presence of other player-characters. On the face of it, this is an ethical
non-event, since it only involves text messages on a screen. However, for
the victim the strong feelings involved were real and Dibbell describes a
distraught individual. This is surely because characters in the game are the
result of investments of meaning and sustained effort on the part of individuals. Players in LambdaMOO nurture their characters over years and
it matters to them how their characters are perceived by other players in
the game world. The violated character had an identity that the player had
constructed carefully and which was maintained with the same diligence
and care that we all use to construct and maintain public selves. It was this

identity that had been violated, rather than something trivial made of text. It was the loss of power the player experienced in relation to their character's identity that made the case a violation. Here we must recall that, according to much of feminist theory, *power*, and not sex or the violation of a physical body, is the issue when rape occurs in the real world. However, most people are reluctant to accept that "cyber-rape" is rape. While the victim may have been distressed, it is unlikely that her trauma was as profound as that of a real rape victim. She could have turned her machine off at any time and not been a witness to the events. This element of choice for the player to engage or not engage and the use of physical equipment involved main-tain an important tension between the two realms, a tension that for most people is handled cognitively – by thinking things out in a way they may not do in other contexts of action. It highlights effectively Hayles's point that the embodiment relation with contemporary technology can actually raise the question of the "missing body" of the reasoning agent. But it also shows that what most people mean by "their body" is still something separate from technology. We recognize technology as a discrete class of objects because it necessitates a particular attitude from us and, as I will argue in the next chapter, this remains true when we "play" with it or involve ourselves in fictions mediated through it.

Related to this is the fact that most contemporary technology projects probably do not involve what Haraway calls "technoscience", but long established scientific and technical knowledge. She acknowledges that the term is political-rhetorical and applies to the developments that are "shiny news" (1997: 55). But even leading edge, experimental techno-logy doesn't raise conceptual challenges to the idea of the human but rather presupposes certain core human qualities. There is a strong tie to the body as a determinant of scale on technology design and the aesthetic desirability of experiences clearly turns on how they involve us physic-ally. The persistence of the molar level (Elster 1985: 31) is not simply a constraint on interface design; however, it is a pervasive feature of all tech-nology design, even in an era when mobile, intangible codes seem to be the ubiquitous medium of technology exchange. This is illustrated by the example of Neil Gershenfeld's "Fab Labs". Gershenfeld is a visionary tech-nologist based at MIT. While others have been captivated by the seeming intangibility of digital codes and the possibilities this opens up, he has been interested in using the mobility of information to enable people to create real objects. He believes that we are about to move beyond the era of personal computing and into the realm of "personal fabrication":

Personal fabrication will bring the programmability of the digital worlds we've invented to the physical world we inhabit. While armies of entrepreneurs, engineers, and pundits search for the next killer computer application, the biggest thing of all coming in computing lies quite literally out of the box, in making the box.

(2005: 17)

His "Fab Labs" are essentially enormously up-graded printers, in the form of high-speed lathes, advanced cutting tools and light engineering equipment, all of which can be controlled through a normal PC. Each Fab Lab costs about $20,000 and personal fabrication technology can, in principle, be used to make almost anything if a digital or mathematical blueprint of it can be found or made[8] and the relevant materials are available. He cites the famous actor, Alan Alda, who claims to have been able to e-mail someone a bicycle. The fact that anyone can intervene and modify designs or even make their own has meant that users of Fab Labs have been able to invent their own designs and produce them, with some interesting results including a coat that produces spikes if people stand too close to the wearer and a device for collecting screams (!). There have also been more significant, practical uses of the technology:

> In the village of Pabal in western India, there was interest in using the lab to develop measurement devices for applications ranging from milk safety to agricultural engine efficiency. In Bithoot, on the bank of the Ganges, local women wanted to do three-dimensional scanning and printing of the carved wooden blocks used for chikan, a local kind of embroidery. Sami herders in the Lyngen Alps of northern Norway wanted wireless networks and animal tags so that their data could be as nomadic as their animals. People in Ghana wanted to create machines directly powered from their abundant sunlight instead of scarce electricity. Children in inner-city Boston used their fab lab to turn scrap metal into sellable jewelry.
>
> (2005: 13)

The Fab Lab may not take off in the way that Gershenfeld anticipates – this will depend upon how the technology plays into contemporary economic and social arrangements. 3-D printers, which are described as "domestic factories capable of producing anything in a lot size of one" (Anderson 2006: 225) and according to economist Chris Anderson, they are becoming more affordable. These developments are a useful reminder that technology is commonly and perhaps fundamentally not merged with the human body or subversive of individual identity, but scaled to meet its requirements and to enhance its operation in the physical world. False teeth and other prostheses remain marginal to our understanding of technology in general, which normally solicits a relatively detached approach aimed at enhancing our grip on the world. Pursuit of relatively lumpy instrumentalities continues to be a vital part of what technology means, regardless of the, possibly transient, seductions of the virtual.

The Agency of Things

A parallel development to feminist "post-humanism" within contemporary theory of technology is actor-network theory (ANT). This theory is mainly associated with the work of Bruno Latour, who has written particularly forceful polemical statements of the ANT position.[9] ANT starts from the constructionist idea that technological artefacts are a product, or effect of interaction of socially relevant agents. It takes this idea a step further, however, by arguing that the same observation applies equally well to humans themselves and, even more importantly, to society. Latour inveighs against other social theorists, including non-ANT constructionists, for whom, he claims, the social is a special kind of substance that causally explains everything else that happens. Latour's view is that the idea of the "social" is a kind of lazy shorthand for things that need themselves to be explained, rather than something that we can take for granted. For ANT, human agents, artefacts and social relations (including "society") require us to explain their emergence and cannot of themselves help us to explain other phenomena.[10] Latour calls previous social theory, which he says has always assumed the existence of society, the "sociology of the social" and contrasts it with ANT's more laborious but ultimately more honest approach. If until now sociology has assumed the existence of society, ANT aims to provide something quite different, which he calls the sociology of association.

This sceptical attitude towards society is different from the attack on the idea that was launched on sociology by Jon Elster and others in the name of methodological individualism. In the 1980s, Elster (1986) argued that sociologists lapsed too readily into citing "society" in explanations and that they overloaded the concept with substantive claims that were fundamentally implausible. His critique targeted the habit that many theorists have of writing about society as if it had properties, tendencies, even attitudes that were irreducible to features of the individuals that made them up. The point of this critique was to insist that if we want to use society as an explanatory variable then we need first to provide an account of the strategic interactions of rational individuals. Latour's scepticism about the social sometimes echoes this critique but, unlike Elster, his objective is not to reconstruct a social concept based on prioritizing human individuals. From the perspective of ANT, the social, or aggregates that make up what we lazily think of as the social can include people, objects, animals or, in principle, anything at all that is connected to anything else. The job of the ANT scholar is to trace out connections and relations between people and things that turn out to be constitutive of the dynamic and shifting field of associations. The social here appears not as a special kind of object or even a specialized domain of enquiry, but only "a very peculiar movement of re-association and re-assembling" (Latour 2005: 7). What ANT researchers are interested in is the networks of association that form between people and objects. Following these makes it possible to identify patterns and regularities that, while in no sense instantiating laws, are constitutive of association. Latour wants to demolish the idea that there is a gulf of knowledge or understanding that separates researcher from researched in the social sciences. He maintains that "it is never the case that the analyst knows what the actors ignore, nor is it the case that the actors know what the observer ignores" (2005: 22) and for this reason we should avoid advancing interpretations of what people seem to be "doing in society". Instead, the role of the social researcher is simply to follow agents and objects as they accumulate connections with one another and build maps of what we see, based on what the actors themselves say. Latour invokes the metaphor of a "snowball", which gathers in size as it rolls along. Social theory, Latour argues, has nothing to add, in terms of interpretative depth or the revealing of hidden significance in events, to the careering accumulation of descriptive data that results from this method. One consequence of such an approach is that the social does not feature in explanations but is itself a kind of effect to be explained. Society lacks independent existence. It may be constituted from quite different materials and be something very different in one study than it is in another. Latour acknowledges that this strains the semantics of the term "social" and for this reason proposes to abandon the concept in favour of the idea of "association". It is already clear, however, that in making the social an effect rather than a driver of constructive processes, ANT also breaks with previous constructionist work on technology. Technological artefacts appear in the networks of ANT not as objects that have been "socially constructed" but alongside other elements in networks of association. From this new perspective, "...it's not technology that is socially shaped, but rather techniques that grant extension and durability to social *ties*..."(2005: 238). In other words, artefacts are, along with people and other objects, constitutive of the snowballs that comprise social networks described by ANT studies.

We are used to affording human agency a certain priority in social analysis. Latour acknowledges that this *seems* perfectly reasonable but argues that it actually obscures our understanding of the processes involved in the constitution of society (2005: 74).

According to ANT, human actions do not require us to interpret them as subject to a special kind of explanation based on "reasons as causes" (Elster 1985: 70–72), for example. They are better understood in the context of interconnections of human objects with other objects in the emergent social field. Their knowledge about their situation and the role this plays in their behaviour are not best-described in terms that centre on individual beliefs, but should rather be seen as distributed throughout the system being described by the ANT analysis:

> Action is not done under the full control of consciousness; action should rather be felt as a whole, a knot and a conglomerate of many surprising sets of agencies that have to be slowly disentangled.
>
> (2005: 44)

In this way Latour resists methodological individualism, even though he shares its scepticism with regard to the independent reality of the social. The behaviour of human objects is to be described in terms that draw on the discursive representations that circulate within the situation, as manifest in the actors' own accounts, and these are a distributed public resource, so to speak.[11] Understanding their distribution means tracing out the patterns of connection in the network and this enables us to characterize some nodes in the network as "localisers", centres of attraction within the social network that draw other points towards them. This echoes Hayles and Haraway's insistence that the notion of a discrete, knowing subject contained in a biological body may be historically superseded:

> Cognitive abilities do not reside in "you", but are distributed throughout the formatted setting, which is not only made of localisers but also of many competence-building propositions, of many small intellectual technologies.
>
> (2005: 211)

Implicit in the last phrase here is the idea that the networks described in this way assign no privileged kinds of connection or agency to human beings. Reasons and knowledge play no special explanatory role in connection to human agency, since technological artefacts are also agents.

The communicative and interactive connections between objects allow us to distinguish between those that conduct lines of force, or meaning without modifying their charges in any way and those that are disruptive of the chain of interconnectedness. Latour calls the first, more passive elements intermediaries while the second, dynamic set are called mediators. Mediators introduce surprises into the social field; their behaviour is never predictable and the meanings or causes that are applied to them – Latour calls these "inputs" – are unreliable predictors of what they will do – "outputs" – or even of how many such actions will result. With mediators "their specificity has to be taken into account every time" (2005: 39). Latour gives a suggestive example to highlight this distinction:

> ... if it breaks down a computer may turn into a horrendously complex mediator while a sophisticated panel during an academic conference may become a perfectly predictable and uneventful intermediary in rubber stamping a decision made elsewhere.
>
> (2005: 39)

The example derives its power because it implies that computers, which are behaviourally the most complex technological artefacts yet invented, are normally passive conduits of meanings and causal forces, while panels comprised of intelligent human beings are normally less predictable and therefore mediators. Latour's point, however, is that we cannot assume such behaviours in advance. They form part of our common sense in relation to situations and common sense is unreliable. In its place, Latour recommends a thoroughgoing relativism as to the significance of actions and events involving people and things, according to which what matters is the place of those actions in the emerging social network and not the idea that they are made of fundamentally different substances, or have different ontologies (2005: 30). Indeed, the distinction between nature and society is historically contingent:

> "Society" and "nature" do not describe domains of reality, but are two *collectors* that were invented together, largely for polemical reasons, in the late seventeenth century.
>
> (2005: 110)

It is intriguing that none of the protagonists in these polemics understood their interventions in these terms, so that Latour here (see also Latour 1993) seems to be engaging in a bit of "critical sociology" of his own, reading sociological meanings into the actions of Bacon and his contemporaries. As we saw in Chapter 3, the increased rationality associated with modernity seems to have been both exaggerated by the moderns (who had political reasons for doing so) and actually present (in the sense that the methods of valid knowledge collection became a matter of sustained reflection and this took on practical consequences). In any case, Latour's assertion that nature and society are contingent frameworks of description that have in some sense run their course is surely exaggerated.

The underlying difficulty here is that it is not clear what it is that ANT actually studies, or why. Why does it describe some associations of objects rather than others? What is its connection with technology and techno-logical artefacts?[12] What is this "charge" that passes between points in a network? Latour argues that just as mediators are constantly translating messages in different languages and codes from diverse sources, so ANT takes its place in this field of intersecting forces and meanings. Its role there is to provide a perspective on these endemic translation processes. However, ANT does not interpret meanings in the associational fields it describes, it merely registers their presence as an effect. Reading ANT we do not gain insights into the meaning of social phenomena for social agents or for us as social enquirers. Just as actors in the field are not caused to act by meaningful reasons, but are merely conduits for order and pattern, so ANT accounts only seek to affect their readers and not to enlighten them. The effect is one of displacement between networks or frames of reference:

> ANT prefers to use what could be called an infra-language, which remains strictly meaningless except for allowing displacement from one frame of refer-ence to the next.
>
> (2005: 30)

Written in a kind of language that operates beneath our semantically loaded, ordinary one, ANT studies are supposed to prompt switches between perspectives or frames of reference. The goal of ANT is not to expose the workings of power or to reveal any truths that were not well known to relevant social actors in the first place, but rather to generate descriptions that do not invoke any social substance. It follows that power too is a concept Latour is prepared to abandon (2005: 64). For ANT, people and objects are no longer separated by conventional disciplinary boundaries or established discursive conventions. Instead, they are positioned on the boundary between these levels of description, in particular between the causal explanations of physical science and meaning-interpretations of the humanities. Indeed, Latour challenges the stability of these distinctions and wants to insist on a third perspective that sits somewhere between them. The problem with ANT as a level of description is that it has no pretensions to be scientific, since Latour denies we can have laws that cover his assemblages, and it lacks any resources with which to handle meaning. Latour invites us to take a leap into the darkness (cf. Feenberg 2002: 52). However, aside from his barbs at the "sociology of the social", he gives us no reasons to follow him, since ANT does not speak to any question or interest that we might take in any given situation. Such interests are essential to motivate any enquiry or the use of any methodological apparatus. The question is, "what will I understand better if I use ANT?" At issue here is not the intersection of people and things in social networks, but the codification of relations between them in interpretative and explanatory discourse. The appropriate way to grasp the relationship between these two levels of description is, as I argued in Chapter 2, in terms of a supervenience relationship. In principle, physics provides a complete account of everything that is there in the universe. Other levels of description, explanation and understanding work within parameters set by this to provide knowledge that corresponds to particular, pragmatic interests humans take in the world (Elster 1985). Sociology does not invoke ghostly entities or substances; it is merely a kind of shorthand tailored to specific needs of the human animal.

Latour's method succeeds not in proscribing a sociology that invokes mysterious substances, but in ruling out the legitimate interpretation of practical motivations and interests that underlie the workings of social power. In sociology of technology, there are at least three discrete standpoints in play. Namely, that of the technician who tells us about the physical behaviour of artefacts; that of social analysis aimed at interpreting the meanings people assign to the artefact in use, and that of normative critique aimed at evaluating actual uses as against possible ones. Collapsing them, as Latour recommends, simply creates confusion. Perhaps most importantly, it begs the question of motivation. After all, networks do not present themselves; we have to look for them. What will motivate our search? Machines, of course, do not need reasons for acting. Latour's suggestion is that the different pragmatic interests (he calls them "collectors") that we take in different kinds of knowledge have ceased to be relevant. That is a matter for historical judgement, but I find it hard to believe that most people will agree with such a drastic conclusion, especially to embrace a de-normativized, non-explanatory social theory cast in a language he himself calls "meaningless".

The Limits of Constructionism

I have argued that when interpreting technology we are obliged to assume that people actively and naturally strive for consistency in their actions and their beliefs about the world and that this involves trying to make things work. Involvement in technology is the consequence of a natural disposition that is certainly stronger in some people than in others and it is true that when institutionalized in differentiated societies it takes on socially specific connotations. It does not, however, in itself require sociological explanation, indeed, it must be viewed as a precondition of interpretation and explanation that people are like this.

It is true that I only say things "work" when they comport with my purposes and enable me to realize my goals through interacting with them. Clearly, the ends of action vary in ways that reflect social and cultural diversity, whereas when we are talking about basic truths like "snow is white", the scope for variation is much less. Nonetheless, using a technology is, like interpreting the statements of a language, something that goes on within certain parameters. There are only so many things that people will want to do with any technology. The human creature has some relatively constant physical characteristics and operates in a world whose fundamental physical properties are constant. When small differences of physical strength between the sexes have been deliberately reflected in technology design and this has contributed to the promotion of ideas of difference to the detriment of females this is clearly regrettable. But in a sense we can only form this judgement because we know that the initial differences *were* minor and that the gains of industrial technology were possible without these consequences. It was always a mistake to identify technology with the masculine in opposition to a feminized nature. Similarly, it would be an error to believe that contemporary technologies overturn our basic categorical distinctions in the direction of the "post-human".

Chapter 3 made the point that people have come up with similar inventions in different times and places, which reflects the fact that technology is a human product and that this sets parameters on its development, so that, for example, people from different cultures have been able to comprehend each other's technologies. These ideas do not contradict the valid point that technology is socially shaped. What they do is set pragmatic limits to the scope of social variation in the development of technology. These pragmatic limits carry normative connotations as well.

An example from the constructionist literature that I think illustrates this point is Donald MacKenzie's (1991) sociology of nuclear missile programmes during the Cold War from 1949 to 1989. MacKenzie's work focuses particularly on the concept of accuracy as a factor in missile design. His historical analysis shows that as a criterion of efficiency and "good" missile design, accuracy varied in significance during this period. One effect of his study is to subvert the impression of nuclear missiles as technology that is inoculated against social influences, answerable only to a narrow, inflexible set of standards derived from science. MacKenzie shows how factors that involved scientific understanding of inertial navigation systems, materials in the bombs and different kinds of propulsion all took on variable significance during the early years of missile design. Crucially, the significance attached to any particular criterion for good design varied depending on the influence wielded by specific social groups and in relation to changes in the world situation, especially strategic geo-politics. For example, in the period immediately after the Second World War the air force exerted a particularly strong influence in nuclear strategy, having been responsible for dropping bombs during wartime. The decision to develop missile delivery systems meant a diversion of resources and a loss of control for them over nuclear strategy. The air force insisted at this time that very stringent parameters on accuracy should be met by missile designers, so that they should not be less accurate than bombers. The criterion, which only allowed a margin of error of about a mile on missiles whose range was intercontinental was almost impossible to meet. It did not stem straightforwardly from considerations concerning the likely target of the bombs themselves in any conflict situation, which might have been either cities (in which case the margin of error could have been very large) or military installations (for which greater precision might have been needed). The demand for accuracy seems to have been more consistently driven by the interests of a particular group than by objective standards. This created a strange situation in the 1950s when missile designers must have breathed a collective sigh of relief that their missiles could be *less* accurate.

The great strength of MacKenzie's account lies in its elaboration of the proximal social factors that influenced the context of the design process and the interaction of these with more technical developments, like the improvement to gyroscopic navigation in the 1950s. Left out of account, though, is the long history of human beings firing projectiles and the implicit, almost natural-historical, concern with getting them to hit targets. There would surely have been a kind of incoherence involved in designing missiles that were not informed at all by accuracy as a criterion – in a sense, such designs could not have been missiles. Adorno's (1973) observation that there is a "universal history" leading from the slingshot to the megaton bomb remains valid, although its darker connotations need to be extirpated – his formulation simply points to anthropological continuities in projectile design and not to a telos of destructive power or motivation. It is true that the goals of a given kind of artefact or tool and the rules of appropriate interaction with it that facilitate effective use are socially acquired and in this sense the constructionist assertion that whether the thing works is just an effect of its social construction is reasonable. However, we can see that it is limited by examining artefacts that do not work. Imagine a bicycle with rusted and twisted spokes in the wheels, in which the wheels are buckled and twisted so that they do not turn within the forks. Imagine that the frame is bent and that it has no saddle, just jagged metal. An object that is in this state clearly does not work. Someone who did not know that it was ever a bicycle, or even what a bicycle was would be able to tell you that this thing does not work. They would, I submit, struggle to find any purpose whatever to be served by it and any purpose they did find would challenge our understanding of the idea of "technology" – they might, for instance, incorporate it into an artwork. On the other hand, a well-maintained bicycle, it is true, could be approached by different groups of people with different objectives in mind. They will be able to invest different meanings in the object and they will, of course, assess whether it works with reference to those meanings. The notion of "working" is primitive in the sense that it is always there whenever we engage with tools. It is most visible when technologists first experiment with an artefact and try to work out what it could be for. This gives rise to technological descriptions of the object, which characteristically emphasize quantity and function, or use. This technological level of description represents a pragmatic orientation to the thing that is guided by a concern to find out what it does. This concern is only minimally informed by an idea of human interests or purposes, which would of course vary according to social and cultural factors. Here the point is about perspective and the interpretation one chooses to apply. A PC user, for example, can continue to work with a dysfunctional computer and can believe that it is "working" because it does not throw out any "error" messages and seems to be behaving as it always has. The same machine viewed from the perspective of a computer hacker or engineer may be infected with a rich assortment of "spy-ware" programmes and viruses. This machine is not "working", or not working well when described in technical terms. The two levels of description operationize different criteria of "working" in connection with this machine. The first is concerned with the flow of energies, behavioural regularities and with a certain formal aesthetics of the artefact. The second is a concern with what I want to achieve now and is socially contingent. Importantly, the first assessment is the more profound of the two, as our user will likely discover in time.

It follows that there may be degrees or kinds of "correctness" in the use of any given artefact, if we accept that social uses supervene on technological ones. In other words, some uses of machines and contraptions actually optimize their performance relative to their potential. This judgement will of course be informed in each case by some knowledge of the purposes to which the technology is put in practice. But in technical discourse this is stipulated minimally and attention turns to the formal structure and properties of the technical artefact itself, whereas in the supervening social discourse use is paramount and seems to constitute the meaning of the technology. Within these two ways of talking about the same object we find different pragmatic interests. As I suggested in the previous chapter, Feenberg understands this semantic ambivalence of technologies in terms of his "dual aspect theory". However, while he associates the two aspects with rival social logics – technical reason and technological rationality, respectively, with the former being contingent on capitalist modernity – they are viewed here as modes of interrelated action and description, that is, in terms of the kind of pragmatism that Habermas has used to re-establish critical theory on a theory of action orientation. Embedding technological interpretation in a specific action orientation enables us to claim that technical and scientific descriptions of technological objects are epistemically privileged and that supervening social purposes and interests are constrained, all the way up, by what we know about our technology from technologists.

Latour argues that critical theory relies on distinctions – between appearance and reality, ideological veneer and sociological substance – that are not valid. The theory is, he says, redundant because the social substance is not there and the tension between seeming consensus and smooth functioning on one side and actual resistance and friction in the social substance is not real, but a figment of the critic's imagination. However, while the critical position might be unfashionable, it is not one that requires any strange metaphysics of social substances or deep tensions for its support. The critical concept of power used here takes as its index not any immanent norm that cannot be realized under capitalist conditions, but the idea of relevant implied counterfactuals pertaining to any technological design. Only a few nostalgics actually bemoan the demise of more transparent and difficult to use interfaces on PCs, for example, but the neglected possibilities do arouse some interest because anyone can see that the interface we have on our PC affects our experience of the information age in important ways. An implied counterfactual – a situation where the interface was less standardized perhaps – gives critical purchase to claims that technology design is shaped by capital often to the detriment of workers and that "user-friendly" interfaces are not always as friendly as they seem. It is perfectly possible to generate a critical sociological account of technology development that cites the involvement of powerful social interests, without invoking any mysterious social substances.

All the theorists discussed here register the changes brought about by digital technology in terms of a radical reconfiguration of the methodological points of departure for the human sciences. In reflecting on this, they concur that one of its implications is a changed relation between the technological and the aesthetic. This has consequences for the methodology of the humanities themselves. Hence, Latour reflects at length on the kind of narrative engine that sociology is – deliberately using ideas from literary theory to problematize the speed with which events occur in sociology's stories. Similarly, Haraway argues that her work is "political-fiction" and is explicit in her conviction that by writing society in a specific way she believes her text can itself exert some transformative effects. Society and politics are discursive constructs, ambiguous between reality and description and it follows that they are subject to modification by imaginative interventions that harness the power of fiction to a politically motivated effort of re-construction. For Hayles, discourse reacts back on bodily experience, reconfiguring our understanding of our own activity, while technology shapes that activity from below. Viewed in this way there is an avowedly aesthetic dimension to the navigation of new technologies and the negotiation of social realities, made manifest for her in a lived tension between embodiment, the lived incorporation of technology into life on one side and the body as something we relate to through processes of intellection on the other. I have argued here that these authors go too far in claiming that our fundamental orderings of the world are altered by the changes they describe. However, their analyses raise the question of the aesthetics of technology in a way that must be addressed and this is the topic of the next chapter.

Technology as Culture

Chapter 3 showed that part of Feenberg's critique of capitalist technology focused on its neglect of an aesthetic dimension in technology design. In this chapter I want to explore this idea. Aesthetic theory concerns the feeling response of the human creature to its environment, not in the sense of emotional feeling but on the basis that there is order in our sensations that makes knowledge itself possible and which works on a level that is analytically discrete from cognition or moral reflection. It follows that technology always involves aesthetics – it feels like something – and technology design has an aesthetic dimension. Even the most horrible industrial machine design had to provide openings, in the form of handles, levers and so on, for the body of its human user at key points in its design.

The aesthetics of technology have become a much-discussed issue in the age of the socially diffuse personal computer (Cubitt 2000; Darley 2000). These machines come with seductive interfaces (Turkle 1995) and they invite their users to respond to the look and feel of their machines as well as their functionality. The previous chapter considered the views of theorists for whom the new experience of aestheticized technology, in which work and play, function and pleasure are merged, calls into question the long-established distinction between the technical and the aesthetic. Contemporary social and media theorists maintain that digital technologies have changed what it feels like to live in modern societies. Digital technology creates a world that feels different to live in and much recent scholarship (Poster 1995, 2006; Urry 2000; Lash 2002) has associated it with a new "social aesthetics". Moreover, they argue this has impacted on politics too because established practices of meaning-communication have given way to encounters with "interactive" technological objects. We no longer read and criticize in order to participate in society, but enter media and become co-participants in "virtual" social spaces. However, much of this literature is quite deterministic in that it overlooks the role of social and cultural forces shaping digital technology and making it the locus of a new aesthetic, as against the idea that digital media simply push society in that direction. I will suggest that this characterization exaggerates the success of attempts to aestheticize technology and misinterprets their implications for social theory. Of central importance in the rise of a so-called digital aesthetic has been the computer game as a cultural form. As traditional aesthetic theory tells us, play is the productive category in the order of aesthetic experience. In this chapter, I use this idea from traditional aesthetic theory to discuss digital aesthetics.

The chapter begins with a discussion of historical changes in technology's aesthetic dimension. The rise of capitalism saw attempts to discipline aesthetic employments of and investments in technology. Enlightenment thinking in the eighteenth century effectively severed the relationship between technology and aesthetic concerns. As we saw in Chapter 3, the emerging capitalist class wanted to separate workers from their tools, which they had decorated and made into personal items with symbolic value, and force them to work with larger, anonymous machines. This assault on earlier aesthetic investments in technology design and the rise of a kind of technology design that is indifferent to aesthetic concerns in the industrial era is central to Feenberg's critique of capitalist technology. The second section "Capitalist De-aestheticization" discusses Feenberg's idea that capitalism suppresses the aesthetic aspect of technology and that re-aestheticization is therefore an essential element in the reform of current technology design principles.

Drawing on Leopoldina Fortunati's analysis of the aesthetics of the mobile phone, the third section "Capitalist Re-aestheticization" suggests that the interface on digital technologies is caught in a problematic zone between technology and aesthetics. Interface design reflects a desire to aestheticize technology but the actual experience of technology use involves the thwarting of this desire. Key to understanding the aesthetic aspirations of contemporary design practices is the notion of virtuality, which is defined in Section 4 "Digital Aesthetics". Contemporary media theory tends to take the virtual as a critical standard for digital culture, even though it is an ideal that remains unrealized in any culturally significant technology designs. In practice, digital artefacts involve people in a way that involves switching between seduction, or immersion in virtual realms and technical analysis, which is essential to using the artefacts and tends to undermine the illusions it projects. That this dynamic is itself pleasurable in an aesthetic sense is evidence of a resurgence of the play principle in culture. In the light of this, I argue that the computer game is paradigmatic for aesthetic experience in digital culture. The concluding section "Neo-Baroque Entertainment Culture" situates the revival of play in theories of "neo-baroque" culture and suggests that technical reasoning plays a central role in our enjoyment of digital entertainment media and that it represents the only path from mere seduction by special effects and awe-inspiring displays to achieving critical distance on and understanding of media products instead of passively consuming them.

Enlightenment and Technology's Aesthetic

Before the enlightenment era and well into the seventeenth and eighteenth centuries, technical artefacts were used to entertain and impress. Indeed, Misa (2004) argues that before the modern, industrial era entertainment uses of technology were always as significant as its use in production and for military purposes. Renaissance technologists like Leonardo da Vinci developed their designs and implemented their ideas in a context where pleasing powerful sponsors and creating spectacles that flattered them were more important than economic productiveness. City-states and courts "were scarcely interested in the technologies of industry or commerce" (Misa 2004: 13). Similarly, Silvia Federici (1995) argues that automata – the attempt to simulate human and other behaviour in devices – precede technological machines with utility in the history of the ancient world (see also Dijksterhuis 1961: 75; Ellul 1964: 45). These kinds of machine peaked in their sophistication and complexity in the seventeenth and eighteenth centuries, just as the machine age in production began to take off. In pre-industrial Europe, technology was more differentiated in its applications where these concerned display, spectacle and what we would think of as entertainment. In its productive applications it remained relatively limited, with agricultural tools and metalworking, for example, having remained unchanged in their essentials for several centuries. This only changed with the confluence of factors that were specific to the eighteenth-century industrial revolution, some of which were discussed in Chapter 3. Prior to this, technology in Europe was shaped by the aristocracy who sponsored technological creativity in that part of the world. According to Maravall (1986) and Ndalianis (2003), the culture of the aristocracy was the baroque, which celebrated complexity and artifice as things to be shown off and enjoyed as displays of virtuosity.

We have seen that there was a growth in enthusiasm for technology in Europe from the seventeenth century onwards, associated with the Enlightenment. However, not all enlightenment thinkers identified technology with scientific progress in this way and not all technologies were seen in the same positive light. Condorcet (1980: 53) and Jean-Jacques Rousseau (1984) were critical of the ways in which the "practical arts" might be used to deceive people and to cultivate what they called "artificial passions". The context of this suspicion of technology was the aristocratic use of technologies in baroque entertainments, which these scholars felt were calculated to mystify and confuse people, rather than to enlighten them. As Barbara Stafford (1994) has pointed out, the French Enlightenment drew an important distinction between frivolous use of technical artifice for entertainments and serious use of telescopes, microscopes and other instruments for the development of learning.[1]

Saisselin (1992) shows that the decline of baroque entertainments was related to the Enlightenment's effort to disparage them as signs of opulence, indulgence and prodigality associated with the aristocracy. Female guests at baroque balls might be seen wearing "grande vieille dames" in their hair. These were mechanical devices that allowed them to raise and lower their hair according to the social status of the person they were talking to – the name reflecting the fact that the device should be lowered in the presence of older females. Such frivolities doubtless motivated Rousseau (1984) to develop his negative portrayal of the historical role of women, according to which it was their attachment to such frippery and display that caused man to lose connection with his inner nature. Modern men, he argued, lived craving the good opinion of others and seeking always to impress them through vain displays. Technology could be used in this context and so it, no less than science, represented an ambiguous gain for humanity. We can read these views as a political reflection on the increasing separation of technology design and use under capitalism. The Enlightenment was the theoretical reflection of the new, bourgeois class and print was the medium through which this reflection was circulated. The new class had little time for entertainments and diversions. They preached discipline and rigour and, as we saw in Chapter 3, they imposed these things on the world with violence. Their social power lent authority to Enlightenment ideas, while technology was appropriated as the preserve of wealthy Europeans. The legitimate uses of technology were defined as work rather than play; education rather than pleasure and frugality rather than prodigality. In this way the social role of technology was narrowed and made subordinate to the needs of a new, capitalist economy. As Saskia Sassen (2006: 85) points out, under capitalism the economy became more foundational for the social structure as a whole. The society that resulted was disciplined, productive and organized on a larger scale and it was in this context that technology became associated with these features.

The pre-eminent philosopher of this movement and the founder of modern aesthetics was Kant. He proposed a tripartite model of human experience, reflecting innate structural features of mind. In his terminology, imagination is the faculty mind has for representing the world of sensory experience, while understanding, or knowledge, is achieved by conjoining representations with innate principles of connection and order. This is the basis of what he calls "determinate judgement", or science. Kant contrasts this with practical or moral reasoning which involves mind interrogating itself for principles that can guide us ethically and hold for all rational beings. If scientific knowledge involves a struggle to comprehend order encountered in experience conceptually, aesthetics is a kind of playful variant of this struggle. Whereas science is successful when it establishes finality, or the ends of things, by identifying their place in the causal order, aesthetic experience is finality without ends. It resists inclusion in the causal order, while playing with the pattern, or form that enables us to produce knowledge. In aesthetic experience we find purpose and order in things that are purposeless and whose order is the order of empty form, or play.

In aesthetic experience, which for Kant is almost exclusively about natural beauty, we find our imagination is pitched against our understanding – we can discern "order and finality" in the object but not its purpose. It seems to be deliberate and yet its purpose is withheld from us. While this might sound annoying, it is a fundamentally pleasurable experience because its resonances bring us to a heightened sense of the harmony that exists between ourselves as authors of these representations and a higher, supersensible, order – the world as it is in itself beyond the reach of our experience. In its *freedom*, the play at the centre of aesthetic experience amplifies our sense of ourselves as free, moral agents. Kant contrasts an intelligent and autonomous exercise of taste, which fathoms this internal movement excited in the subject, with judgements that are based merely on superficial responses to objects:

> Taste that requires an added element of *charm* and *emotion* for its delight, not to speak of adopting this as the measure of its approval, has not yet emerged from barbarism ...

> A judgement of taste which is uninfluenced by charm or emotion ... and whose determining ground is, therefore, simply finality of form, is a *pure judgement of taste*.

> (1961: 65)

True aesthetic judgement centres on the form that solicits this internal play of the faculties. Beautiful objects have the paradoxical form of a purposeless finality; they are supremely well-executed, delightful things and yet we cannot see any purpose in the perfection. They present us with a form so precise that it seems to be mathematically ordered, yet we cannot conceive a formula adequate to describe them. This is why beautiful things "play" with our faculties. Kant puts play at the centre of aesthetic experience, noting that, "...play of every kind...is attended with no further interest than that of making the time pass by unheeded" (1961: 166). While it is internal to the subject, the kind of play Kant has in mind is intellectual but is based on the very same play we associate with fun:

> Music...and what provokes laughter are two kinds of play with aesthetic ideas, or even with representation of the understanding, by which, all said and done, nothing is thought. By mere force of change they are yet able to afford lively gratification. This furnishes pretty clear evidence that the quickening effect of both is physical, despite its being excited by ideas of the mind, and that the feeling of health, arising from a movement of the intestines answering to that of play, makes up that entire gratification of an animated gathering upon the spirit and refinement of which we set such store.
>
> (1961: 198–9)

Kant identifies this play with music, gardens and nature, but has little to say about the visual arts or entertainment of his time. This reflects a bias of the Enlightenment against those things, which seemed to be a distraction of the imagination, pulling it away from its true role in servicing cognition with representations of the world and (ab-)using scientific understanding to achieve this. Nature, in contrast, could be legitimately contemplated with awe and represented in the mind's eye for pleasure's own sake, since this was an appropriate response to God's work. This pious attitude set the ground for both the modern understanding of aesthetic experience and the denial of any aesthetic dimension to technology characteristic of industrial capitalism.

Capitalist De-Aestheticization

Although Misa claims that "gold-bricked locomotives" were more important motives than profit for nineteenth-century imperialism (2004: 127), there is consensus in most of the literature on industrial technology that it is lacking in positive aesthetic qualities, compared to other historical technologies. After making the alarming observation that in the sixteenth century "there was an absence of reasoning concerning human action" (1964: 38) Jacques Ellul maintains that technology design at that time exhibited greater diversity, which,

> ... cannot be explained as a manifestation of a technical enquiry. The modific-ations of a given type were not the outcome of calculation or of an exclusively technical will. They resulted from aesthetic considerations. It is important to emphasise that technical operations, like the instruments themselves, almost always depended on aesthetic preoccupations. It was impossible to conceive of a tool that was not beautiful.
>
> (1964: 72)

Similarly, Lewis Mumford (1947) and Neil Postman (1993) argue that industrial technology marks a decisive break in the history of technology at precisely the level of its aesthetics. Yet, even during the industrial era, aesthetic concerns did not disappear entirely. Noble (1984) describes how workers in the machine tools industry would cut pleasing curves and extraneous decoration into their pieces, before the process was auto-mated, and uses this to highlight how scientific technology deprives workers of control over the labour process, and Braverman (1974: 10) notes that technology played an important symbolic role in neutralizing the revolutionary aspirations of US workers in the twentieth century. There it was the scale and complexity of technology that created an effect, namely, awe and pacification. According to Feenberg, capitalist technology is uniquely ugly because it has not been "re-contextualised".

As we saw in Chapter 3, Feenberg argues that all technology involves a kind of initial violence, "primary instrumentalisation", which is a consequence of taking an instrumental approach to the world. In pre-capitalist cultures, this initial phase is followed by "secondary instru-mentalisation", which involves a re-investment of meaning in the technological objects created:

> The reduction of the technical object to primary qualities is compensated to some extent in all societies by aesthetic and ethical investments that enrich it once again and adapt it to its environment.
>
> (2002: 180)

When medieval craftsmen decorated their tools they were re-aestheticizing the world they had violated in the first place and giving their artifice and its products a new context that compensated for the loss of the natural one in which the raw materials of labour and technology were found. This made up for the force with which they were wrested from their finding places in nature. What distinguishes capitalist technology is its historically unique failure to "re-aestheticise" technology, to compensate nature, so to speak, for the violence of primary instrumentalization. A medieval tool signified the abilities of its possessor, his social standing and his place within the cosmic order and would be decorated accordingly. The ugliness of capitalist industrialism traces to a lack of such symbolic meaning which is itself a function of the narrowed horizon under which technology develops – the hegemonic technological rationality discussed in Chapter 4. There has been a diminution of meaning in capitalist technology because the cultural horizon on technology design under capitalism imposes the idea that technology is there solely to amplify productive capacity and to maximize efficiency. Efficiency is narrowly defined according to a simple principle, namely that the most output be achieved for the least input of energy and other costs, such as skills. This parsimonious definition of technology is essential to capitalism and it is responsible for the negative experience of technology that most people had under industrial capitalism. Only under capitalism are tools valued exclusively for their instrumental efficacy in productive processes. No care is paid to the appearance of industrial machinery and minimal attention given to what it feels like to use. The social pressures driving the design and construction of factory plant can be summed up as the capitalist drive to control labour and maximize profits. This is why Feenberg argues there is an inherent compatibility between capitalism and primary instrumentalization (1999: 183).

However, the situation is not irretrievable. The truth about technological efficiency is subject to challenge and renegotiation. Alternative truths about the best way to use a technology can be put forward and those excluded from the original design choices can find a "margin of maneouvre" from within which they can change technology design. This involves an aesthetic dimension whereby transformations in technology design make technology more meaningful and allow for it to be more harmoniously integrated into human affairs. This should not be confused, Feenberg says, with mere packaging:

> ...modern societies...are unique in distinguishing production from aesthetics and ethical regulation. They are heedless of the social insertion of their objects, substitute packaging for an inherent aesthetic elaboration, and are indifferent to the unintended consequences of technology for human beings and nature. Various system crises result from this artificial separation of technique, ethics, and aesthetics.
>
> (Feenberg 2002: 180)

Redressing this separation and overcoming the crisis tendencies are to be achieved through a re-aestheticizing of technology. Feenberg identifies this as the most important task of critical theory of technology and relates it directly to environmentalism. The environmental degradation that results from modern industrial technology is to be addressed not through a return to more natural ways of living, but through new design strategies that seek out "synergisms by which the environment can be enlisted in the structure of appropriate technology" (2002: 190). However, as I argued in Chapter 3, Feenberg's association of technical reason and capitalism constitutes a residual substantivism in his theory that does not need to be there. The point is that a narrow concept of efficiency combined with the violence of capitalist socio-economic relationships are cultural encasings of technology, just as decorated tools with personal significance are. Technical reason is not, in itself, intrinsically more compatible with one than it is with the other. Romantic critics of capitalism have repeatedly aligned the two, at least since Rousseau, but technical reason – the attitude of trying to puzzle out a practical solution and manipulating objects in the world to secure new affordances – is not inherently violent, unless you hold that any action is violent. Because it is experimental and tends to find new possibilities, technical reason will always be a potential source of instability in a culture, which is why some societies have legislated to inhibit it, but the latter is a restriction on freedom that should be abhorred, just as specifically capitalist uses of technology have frequently been objectionable. In my view, this becomes important if we want to distinguish between packaging and aesthetic substance in contemporary technical designs.

Capitalist Re-Aestheticization

It is intriguing that digital technology, once associated with "scientific" management and with a corresponding de-aestheticization of tools now opens out onto a new era of aestheticized machines. A good example of this is the mobile phone. In her study of mobile use in Italy, Leopoldina Fortunati shows that mobiles "have become 'fashionable' by being incorporated into the aesthetic management of the body's visual field" (2002: 54). This includes a certain discretion about revealing and using the phone in public, which balances modesty and display, and covers the extent to which people use their phone, which is a matter of style as well as economy. Propelling this incorporation of the mobile into self-presentation is a dialectic of fascination and revulsion that attaches to the device as an artificial entity that is worn like clothing, close to the body. Mobile aesthetics involve technology as a sign of domination over nature (we extend our communicative range) and of more artificiality (there is something superficial, or inauthentic about all gadgets). The mobile signifies technological solutions to problems of distance and co-ordination, but at the same time its presence reminds us that these problems still exist. Its artificiality signifies its imperfection and a kind of pre-existing dis-harmony that it cannot fully address. This tension or oscillation within the sociological meaning of the mobile positions it in a strange relationship to art and traditional aesthetic theory:

> By coming closer to the body, technology is in some way sucked inside the clothing and thus fashion itself, which is such a powerful vehicle for spreading art today. Technology must, therefore, reconcile itself with art.
>
> (Fortunati 2002: 58)

The reconciliation Fortunati has in mind concerns the place of the artefact in culture and, in particular, the capitalist society that distorts technology development. Fortunati argues that this is unique to the mobile because of its relation to the body. However, her argument can be extended to incorporate digital technology more generally. The reason for this is that, in a sense, digital technology is always open and its meaning unresolved in a way that is, perhaps, historically unprecedented.

As we saw in Chapter 2, a defining feature of technology is that it closes over on its own inner workings. Part of what makes a desirable tool is that as users we do not need to be concerned with how it works in order to use it to achieve our purposes. It is a tool because it abbreviates certain courses of action so that to illuminate the room, for example, I throw the light switch and do not need to model the behaviour of electricity, filaments or gases in bulbs. The computer interface is an attempt to close the box on the computer, to withhold its operations from further scrutiny in order that the machine can become a device (Borgmann 1984). However, what is distinctive about the microcomputer is that there was (and perhaps is) no firm consensus on what it is actually for. More than thirty years into the "computer revolution", new uses for home computer technology are still being discovered. Each requires subtle alterations to the interface of the machine and its operating system needs to be sufficiently flexible to accommodate this endless differentiation, while at the same time not tipping over into becoming something too challenging for the "ordinary user" to cope with. This is the technical problematic of interface design (Norman and Draper 1986). In the course of its development, however, the interface on personal computing technology has been caught in the crossfire of competing social interests. Interface designers found that their position was greatly enhanced during the multimedia revolution in personal computing of the mid-1990s. Their role has been to come up with a universal model that will make the computer a machine that can be open to all future possibilities, while presenting those possibilities in a way that most people can relate to. This has led to a series of "visionary" interventions, including Negroponte's (1995) thesis of ubiquitous computing, whereby the interface simply disappears into the environment, which now understands natural language and becomes responsive to our commands. Also of note is Brenda Laurel's (1993) notion that the interface should resemble a drama, or a theatrical production in which interface elements are players and the user is a kind of director who manages the script and oversees the production. Here too, the goal is to make the interface disappear, so that users do not feel that they are dealing with technology at all, but merely taking advantage of available affordances. These idealizations of the interface position it in the space between technology and aesthetics, identified by Fortunati.

The tensions in this space and the contradictions that beset the social construction of the interface have been overlooked in much contemporary media theory. For example, Mark Poster (1995) accepts uncritically the design principle that the ideal interface would be one that simply merged with the environment, becoming entirely transparent. According to this vision, human beings interact directly with information, or data structures, without ever having to contemplate them under demanding technical descriptions:

> With representational machines such as the computer the question of the interface becomes especially salient because each side of the human/machine divide now begins to claim its own reality: on one side of the screen is Newtonian space, on the other, cyberspace. Interfaces of high quality allow seamless crossings between the two worlds, thereby facilitating the disappearance of the difference between them and thereby, as well, altering the type of linkage between the two. Interfaces are the sensitive boundary between the human and the machinic as well as the pivot of an emerging set of human/machine relations.
>
> (Poster 1995: 21)

Poster's "high quality" interfaces offer their users simulated environments that instantiate "post-modern" aesthetics. From this point of view, there is no longer any distinction between simulated and real, we pass between the two worlds without even noticing. However, it is an error to assume that "high quality" interfaces can be defined in this way because the seamless interface is only one design standard and it embodies particular interests. Moreover, the invisible interface is as yet an unattainable fantasy far removed from the daily experience of most users of digital artefacts.

Claims have often been made for the aesthetic virtues of particular kinds of technology. According to Bijker and Pinch (2002: 89), one nineteenth-century enthusiast of the high-wheeled bicycle argued that it "sharpened the senses" and made for "the ultimate aesthetic experience". Among the anthropologically given traits of the human animal, play and its pleasures are present in all cultures (Huizinga 1950; Caillois 1958). It is true that the bicycle is not inherently about speed and excitement, but a culture that did not find these things in it through play, even if only to suppress them is hard to imagine. Similarly, the microcomputer has taken its place in a culture of interpretation and become a plaything. It is well documented (Levy 1984; Markoff 2006; Turner 2006) that the idea of personal computing, which gave birth to microcomputers for the domestic market, came from the 1960s counterculture. For early hackers, the appeal of computing lay in the complexity of the activity. They derived pleasure from studying computer behaviour at the hardware level, mapping this behaviour through the use of mathematics and using their understanding to try and achieve effects that no one else had thought of. It is difficult to see how such activities could be a source of pleasure unless we understand them in terms of the tradition of puzzle-solving play (Himanen 2002). These early experiences of computer use set in train a dialectic between the rigours of puzzling out mathematical problems on one side and responding to and producing new effects at the interface on the other. Sherry Turkle (1984) interprets this in terms of competing computational aesthetics. Hacking involves instrumental reason as applied to the resources of the machine, while a "user" aesthetic involves relating to the computer as a source of simulations that are manifest at its interface. In practice, each of these orientations presupposes the other and using a computer involves shifting between the two ways of experiencing the machine. We are often "thrown" in computer use, during which time we can focus on our task – writing an essay, or building a library of tunes – but occasionally we must contemplate the fact that it is a computer we are using. We all do "housekeeping" operations, like making sure our anti-virus software is up-to-date, and in these processes we learn about the machine. As ideal types, hackers set great store by their ability to solve a problem in the most elegant and economical way with regard to the machine's resources, while gamers and ordinary users enjoy the way the machine looks and feels and relate to it as a metaphorically constructed "environment", but these are idealizations and the reality for most of us lies in the more messy area in between. This means computers are technological, on the definition put forward earlier, and aesthetic. They are caught in the tension described by Fortunati – we wish they were not technology but every step taken towards eliminating their technical aspect only creates new manifestations of their incorrigibly technical character. Interface design is contested in practice by a range of social constituencies (open source programmers, game modders,[2] hacktivists, digital artists) who use computers in a way that is more consistent with a "modernist" aesthetic, which draws out and makes explicit the connection between autonomous creativity with computers and difficult, demanding work at the level of coding the machine. This modernist aesthetic refuses the idea of "seduction" by the interface and advances an alternative vision that involves users reclaiming some of the cognitive burdens of computer use and incorporating instrumental reasoning about how the machine works into creative processes (Kirkpatrick 2004).

Viewed in this way, the user-friendly interface represents a problematic, even stalled re-aestheticization of the machine. Diffusion of the personal computer goes on under a rhetoric of making the technology available to people. It projects the computer as a source of spectacle and visual entertainment. At the same time, however, we can see that much interface design is actually concerned with inhibiting the free and experimental use of computers by individuals and marginal groups. This is related to the use of interface design to maintain proprietary controls over machines, networks and so-called virtual spaces.[3] What we see in contemporary technology design and interface design in particular is a capitalist re-aestheticization, or a deliberate re-investment of technology with aesthetic values. It is no longer true that re-aestheticization is left entirely to chance, in the sense of workers engraving their own industrial tools as discussed in Chapter 4, since design is now self-consciously aesthetic, concerned with making machines that are attractive and even environmentally friendly. At the same time, this re-aestheticization is stymied and incomplete.

Digital Aesthetics

In different ways, Poster (1995, 2006), John Urry (2000) and Scott Lash (2002) have maintained that the informational form differs from printed text, narrative or discourse in that it abolishes the distance between author and recipient that was essential to critique. The difference is a function of changes in the aesthetics of reception. Whereas older modes of transmission maintained the "modernist" distinction between reader and text, information works directly on the recipient, reconfiguring them in the fashion of a computer programme flipping electronic bits in a machine. This machinic mode of experience does not allow the user to detach themselves and apply critical standards drawn from outside the experience. There is neither a transcendent source of critical ideas that might be applied, nor a tension immanent to the experience between its human and machinic components. Rather, in the confrontation with new media objects people are actively involved in reconfiguring themselves and the objects, a process Lash evocatively characterizes as an active extrusion of human mental content (2002: 59). The cultural context for this is what Hayles (1999) calls the "post-human", or Latour's levelling of the field of relations between humans and things, discussed in the previous chapter. Because our engagement with new media objects is as much a story of their engagement with us, the role of critical reflection in understanding these processes is diminished in favour of an aesthetic assessment. What matters is less the development of a rational critique than measuring the kinds of affective engagement, or what it feels like to be a participant in the "second media age" (Poster 1995). This approach is informed by Walter Benjamin's theory of aesthetics as a channel in the distribution of social power.

Benjamin was associated with the first generation of critical theorists, Adorno and Horkheimer. In his essay "On the work of art in the age of mechanical reproduction" (1968), written in 1936, he argues that aestheticized art, in the sense of art that stimulates Kant's essentially private play of subjective feelings, is over. Contemporary aesthetic experience works on the public surfaces of its audiences rather than their inner spiritual depths. However, notwithstanding his friend Adorno's critique of this situation as heralding a new barbarism, Benjamin argues that it is not a catastrophe. In film, we find that visual pleasure ceases to be merely contemplative and becomes instead married to critical intelligence. Films must be interrogated and not merely consumed for their meanings to be extracted. Film watching necessitates film criticism and this means that the aesthetics of the medium cannot simply be about enhanced social control or propaganda. Film quite literally opens up a new perspective, so that for the Soviet moviemaker and 1920s pioneer of cinematic form Dziga Vertov, the movie camera would be to the social sciences what the microscope and telescope had been to the physical sciences – revolutionary extensions of the visual.[4] What he called the "kino-eye" was a new experience of the visual in which critical intelligence informed our use of the visual field. Understood in this way the movie was reconfiguring the aesthetic orientation of twentieth-century humans – in the direction of enlightenment. A common theme in writing on digital media is that it too introduces a new dimension to visual experience. This is related to the idea of virtuality.

There are three meanings of "the virtual" in the literature (see Shields 2003; Ryan 2001; and Hayles 1997). The first concerns the prevailing sense that codes matter more than material substances. While codes always require instantiation in some material interface, they are more important in determining the character of the experience we derive than the interface material. This sense that there is a pattern that conditions our experience gives rise to the idea of intangible determinants of experience that was not culturally salient before. The second sense of virtuality involves the technical practice of Virtual Reality (VR). Head-sets, gloves and even full body apparatus exploit the fact that codes are mobile to develop illusions that deceive all of the senses at once in a co-ordinated fashion, realizing Bacon's vision of a complete "deceit of the senses" described in Chapter 3. Here virtuality describes the resultant sense of a world that is fully present in that no human creature with a working sensory apparatus could tell the difference between the real world and the illusory one. A third meaning of the term arises in connection with the visual arts, especially the history of perspective. Since the discovery of linear perspective in the Renaissance, art works have presupposed the position of a privileged viewer (cf. Berger 1974). Visual spectacles and displays have been constructed with this viewer in mind. The same principle informed the development of electronic visual media, including film and television. The kino-eye was a prosthetic extension of the human eye that made this privileged point mobile and enabled it to see social phenomena more clearly. However, according to Grau (2000), virtual art introduces a new principle within this history:

> The technical idea that is virtual reality now makes it possible to represent space as dependent on the direction of the observer's gaze: the viewpoint is no longer static or dynamically linear, as in the film, but theoretically includes an infinite number of possible perspectives.
>
> (2000: 16)

It does not privilege and is not aimed at any single perspective and instead can be inspected from many points of view. With the virtual art object the viewer enters the work and inspects it from the inside. The visual affords us access to an experiential object with an infinite number of possible perspectives, corresponding to where we choose to position ourselves.

John Urry grasps the notion of virtuality in his description of the holographic image, which he says embodies a visual logic that is increasingly salient in our experience. He positions the hologram as a kind of metaphor for post-modernity:

> In pre-modern societies predominant metaphors were those of various animals, as well as different kinds of agricultural work (many are still powerful today). In modern societies predominant metaphors have been those of

the clock, various types of machinery and the photographic lens. While for post-modern societies the hologram would be a productive metaphor. Holography is based upon non-sequentiality, the individual-whole relationship and complexity. Information is not located in a particular part of the hologram. Rather, any part contains, implies and resonates information of the whole... The language of cause and effect is inappropriate since the connections are simultaneous and instantaneous.

(2000: 123)

What Urry has in mind is the rapidity of information transmission, which with digital-networked computers becomes instantaneous and global. Information present here and now on my computer screen is in principle available anywhere else to anyone else on the planet. The holographic image conveys this idea and symbolises how, for Urry and others, we have moved into a new perceptual regime or paradigm (Kirby 1997) under which everything can be made present to the senses in all of its aspects. As we saw in the previous section "Capitalist Re-aestheticization", the notion of the virtual as marking a new kind of media object, which users enter and work with from within as if it were co-extensive with the natural world is one that guides interface designers too. However, as a central metaphor the holograph misses the stymied and contested character of digital media aesthetics, which is reflected in the fact that very few of our encounters with digital artefacts actually incorporate anything like the holographic or the virtual. It also reduces agency to a form of spectatorship (however full and instantaneous) and thereby misses the central role of play and experimentation in digital aesthetics. In the rest of this section I argue that the computer game, and not the hologram, is the best metaphor for contemporary culture. Just as films had to be interrogated and not merely consumed, so most peoples' experience of digital artefacts involves active, critical engagement rather than a distinctive deployment of the visual sense. The uncritical stance taken by contemporary theory towards the hegemonic interface runs the risk of collapsing social theory into affirmation of what Benjamin would have called the aestheticization of politics – the deliberate use of aesthetic effects to steer peoples' thinking as part of a strategy of three-dimensional power. As a Marxist, Benjamin called for the politicization of aesthetics. Uncritical acceptance of the "virtual" interface as unproblematic mediator of the information society leads contemporary media theorists to argue that contemporary politics is a question of negotiating new identities rather than seeking emancipation and autonomy. The political implications of this surrender to a "post-modern" version of digital aesthetics will be explored further in the next chapter.

There is an emerging consensus on the cultural importance of the computer game. For Kline, Dyer-Witherford and de Peuter, games are the "ideal commodity of contemporary capitalism" (2003: 76; cf Kerr 2006: 1). As left-wing media theorists they denounce the form for its "militarised masculinity", its "promotion of branding and marketing aimed at children" and its failure to really experiment with the possibilities opened up by computer technology for educational applications.[5] Notwithstanding this, the common computer game is a better metaphor for most people's experience of digital culture than the virtual world or hologram. Kline *et al*'s critique neglects the defining feature of the computer game as a cultural form, which is play. Play is anthropologically primitive, linking human nature to that of animals (Huizinga 1950).[6] Games are rule governed systems that structure play without negating its essentially purposeless character. Games differentiate and organise play and their degree of complexity can even be seen as indexical for 'civilization' (Caillois 1958). The history of games provides the context within which computer games should be understood. Of all social and cultural forms, the game enjoys a privileged relationship to play and the computer game extends and updates this tradition.

In computer games critical engagement with the interface and the computer as a machine with comprehensible, technical rules of behaviour is the norm. Gamers are drawn in by the quality of a game's graphics and may be interested in its storyline, but in the course of playing the game they engage with it as a puzzle to be solved. Gamers use technical knowledge and understanding of computer behaviour to work out when a solution applied to one game will probably work for another, regardless of the story or the visual 'world' projected by the game. A recent survey of gamers in Britain by the British Board of Film Classification showed that game play requires "active engagement" (BBFC 2006: 34), with players reporting that they "have to concentrate". This aspect of intelligent puzzle-solving is more important for most gamers than stories in games or the visual representational qualities of their fictional worlds. Indeed, players commonly lose sight of these things altogether in the course of engaging with the specific challenges associated with intense periods of game play. This extends to portions of game content that seem, to an observer who is not playing the game, to involve violence. For gamers, the violence in games is less worrying than in films because "film images are more 'real' than computer graphics and film creates a more compelling illusion" (2006: 13). In other words, video games do not invite people into seductive illusions, but rather use the power of graphical images and the appeal of being able to take control of a character or situation to get their attention. Once players are engaged games challenge them to use their cognitive skills to solve

puzzles. Viewed in this way, computer games are aestheticised technology that reminds us of, perhaps even taunts us with, the distance that
still exists between technology and art, work and pleasure, so long as
we do not change the economic and social system within which digital
technologies take their place. The cultural significance of the video game
may be that it highlights the fissures and failures of the virtual as a design
principle.

A number of theorists have argued that computer games involve
'presence' for players, invoking the sense of being able to enter the
media object, or interacting with it, as a central aspect of play. Some
conjoin this description of play with the notion of immersion in a 'game
world' as an implicit critical standard. Virtuality works here as a kind of
guiding myth informing the development of the medium. Consequently,
although games "fall well short of being truly immersive" (King and
Krzywinska 2006: 111), this is only because, like cinema before the advent
of talking movies, they have not yet realized their full potential in relation to their guiding myth.[7] Games and devices deployed to construct
games are assessed in terms of how well they facilitate player immersion
in game worlds. Hence, King and Krzywinska argue that different on-
screen perspectives offered by games "correlate" with different degrees of
player "presence" and conclude a discussion of the different perspectival
devices employed in games by noting the compromised character of the
linear perspective (2006: 101) offered by many games on their fictional
environments. This is held to undermine the sense of immersion, or the
feeling of psychological absorption, in games and they suggest that it is
a failing. Presence involves being able to assume a potentially infinite
number of perspective points within an illusion, with the corresponding
sense that one's physical centre is *in* the illusion. However, this is not
a good description of gamer experience. Normative concerns of video
game scholarship aside, there are few if any games that actually measure
up to virtuality, or the idea of a fully immersive environment as an
ideal and this does not seem to inhibit their success as a medium.
The cultural significance of the computer game rests rather with the
experience of play. As argued above, aesthetic form exerts the hold it
does over successive generations of humans primarily because it too
works with the playful and the humorous. The aesthetic qualities of
the computer game do not involve a new 'virtual' employment of the
visual, but centre rather on the role of play. It is because they facilitate
play and excite our sense of form that computer games are compelling and just as in traditional artworks, straightforward literal readings
of their content are out of place. Ironically perhaps, these principles
were probably best grasped up by Kant in his comments on play and
form.

Neo-Baroque Entertainment Culture

Angela Ndalianis (2003) includes computer games in her idea of a 'neo-baroque' entertainment culture. Following the 1930s art theorist and historian of the first baroque, Henri Focillon (1992), she argues the baroque is characterised by a proliferation of form and artifice. In baroque works, technique and ostentation displace meaning and significance. Like the Renaissance, the baroque was not only a movement within the arts. As Saisselin puts it:

> In using the term *Baroque* we mean to designate not only the architecture of Bernini, or an open pictorial space and the contrast of light and dark, but a civilization that can be associated with the period of absolute monarchy, with an alliance of church and state to maintain the hierarchical structure of society, and even with economic mercantilism.
>
> (1992: 3)

In other words, it is a cultural totality that overlaps with the late Renaissance and with the early modern period. It is associated specifically with monarchical absolutism and the pre-capitalist economic formation that was present in Europe until well into the seventeenth century. In this context, physical pleasures, especially visual pleasures, were highly esteemed. Stafford refers to "rolicking pastimes, innocent and not so innocent sensual pleasures, outdoor and indoor spectacles, aristocratically feminine masquerades, and gentlemanly blood sports" (1994: 23) all of which were characteristic of the lifestyle of the baroque nobility.

The defining form of the first baroque was the labyrinth and this form resurfaces now at the end of modernity.[8] Neo-baroque works involve the reader physically shaping media texts. Choices we make determine the next set of possibilities in the fictional narrative. Ndalianis stresses the role of the consumer in co-creating the artefact thus: "... the baroque aspects of labyrinthicity emerge when the construction of the labyrinth itself ... becomes a significant source of the work's meaning" (2003: 86).[9] There is an excess of form that overwhelms and engulfs the user while the fictional meaning or representational aspects of the work recede. For example, in TV series like NBC's *Lost,* or the many sequels and remediations of the *Alien* series, or the multiple iterations of some computer games like *Final Fantasy,* the tendency is for huge, sprawling diegetic worlds in which maintaining consistency becomes a real problem for authors and producers. Ndalianis argues that the pleasure people take in these productions is such that they accept inconsistencies. There is no "privileged" or correct reading of a neo-baroque work, just different navigations, and since each reading is discrete and separate from the rest, there is no need to look for coherence. She invokes structuralist ideas of syntagm and paradigm to make sense of this new kind of reading. Neo-baroque texts are made up of syntactic elements, which, read as components of a traditional, linear narrative would be unsatisfying, probably shallow. If we are to derive anything other than shock value or other surface effect we to re-arrange them and establish what Ndalianis calls paradigmatic settings for the syntactic elements. She writes,

> Neo-baroque narration depends on folds that also enfold the audience. The film's story (its syntagmatic layer) remains stagnant and cliché; the media-literate spectator, however, quickly shifts to the exciting journey offered on a paradigmatic level, at which he or she must actively engage in the intertextual, labyrinthine connections that exist across this axis of meaning production.
>
> (2003: 79)

For audiences this involves engagement with the syntagmatic level of a narrative through fragments that disclose something of the texture and feel of the fiction and later identification with its paradigmatic level, which is imaginatively constructed by them out of these fragments. The fragments may be derived from diverse sources, including different media platforms and this is part of the appeal of the neo-baroque artefact.

However, this analysis is unsatisfactory because, while it is certainly correct to argue that there is a relation between the individual scenarios that make up a game and its totality as a fiction, the way these connections are drawn out involves effort and takes the player into a set of experiences that make the fictional meaning a secondary property of the work. Ndalianis is wrong to suggest that people accept inconsistencies and incoherence in these different manifestations of the story world. On the contrary, the *avant-garde* of the interactive co-creating audience is hunting incoherence down. We see this in the innumerable "fan-sites" where enthusiasts of games, TV programmes and other neo-baroque productions analyze them in detail. A particularly good example of this concerns *Lost*. When this show was first broadcast in 2004–6, websites mushroomed as people experimented with different hypotheses that might make the events depicted come out as coherent. Hypotheses ranged from the idea that everything in the show was part of one character's delusion, to the suggestion that all the characters were dead and in a kind of "limbo" between heaven and hell. The discussions were fixated on the fine points of each plot line and were relentlessly logical in their pursuit of consistency and order. By substituting a post-structuralist theory of signification for a sociological exploration of the dynamics of neo-baroque "reading", Ndalianis effaces the nature of agency in the neo-baroque and overlooks the political significance attached to the enormous amount of effort that goes into each of these readings and the desire for coherence that motivates them. Implied here *is* a novel experience of reading, but it involves work that is done by audiences to establish consistency and eliminate incoherence from even the most ridiculous fictions. The relation between part and whole in these forms is not fully grasped by Ndalianis's theory of signification.

A game like *Resident Evil 4* (Capcom 2002), for example, involves exploration of a vast series of unpleasant locations. To progress through the game requires intense concentration on elements within the game that often stretch and undermine the plausibility of the fictional world projected by the game graphics. For example, in one sequence we find our character in a ruined church surrounded by (and populated with) murderous zombie-like creatures. The only way out appears to be through the graveyard, but there is no obvious exit, just a wall and facing it a podium. Positioning your character on the podium you are offered a view of what looks like a children's puzzle. You have to put symbols in the correct order to open a secret passageway. Solving this puzzle can take hours, yet viewed as a fiction analogous to film, we are supposed to believe our character is still standing there in the grave-yard. It is obvious that engagement with the puzzle here disperses and supplants any concern with the game as fiction (Juul 2005: 139). In many cases this puzzling out extends to using cheat codes and phys-ical manipulation of the game hardware. In *Metal Gear Solid* (Konami 1998), for instance, solving one puzzle involves unplugging a controller and switching it to a different port (Galloway 2006: 34–5). Players of *Pokemon Diamond* or *Pokemon Pearl* (Game Freak, Incorp. 2007) on the Nintendo DS machine have to work out that different creatures are avail-able for capture depending on which Gameboy cartridge is inserted in the socket of the machine that is not (supposedly) in use at the time. The concentrated state of mind (and body) associated with solving the puzzle becomes the trigger that opens up the next part of the game. For King and Krzywinska, the discovery of new seen environments in this way is a kind of release that corresponds to the aesthetic element in gaming. But the aesthetics of the game incorporate the entire process, something Bogost grasps better through his notion of "simulation fever". Players, he says, move between accepting the game as a simulated or virtual world and interrogating its fundamental properties. This process " . . . insinuates seriousness back into play and suggests that games help us expose and explore complicated human conditions, rather than offering mere inter-ruptions and diversions" (Bogost 2006: 136). Playing computer games involves racing through a series of puzzles overlaid on puzzles that, once solved, open out onto a growing sense of pattern or, in aesthetic terms, form. Game scholarship that downplays the tensions and contradictions of this process and reads games in terms of their stories is really only engaging with their "packaging" (Feenberg), or their "charm" (Kant) and overlooks their aesthetic aspect. Players experience the form of a game often without really thinking very much about its story content or its "fictional world". The excitement is not dissimilar to that of riding a bicycle too fast.

It is primarily as playful medium (a game) that the computer, having been itself socially shaped, is in turn, re-coding contemporary entertainment culture. This can be seen in innovations to mainstream media productions, where digital media technologies are deployed alongside analogue ones to make available new kinds of narrative access to fictional worlds. The key difference between these narratives and those of traditional, print media is not a loss of critical distancing on the part of readers, but rather that the media objects have to be physically assembled, or configured by their audiences (Galloway 2005: 13; Bogost 2006: 121; Kerr 2006: 119–121). This process involves both critical intelligence and physical action. The skill involved is not that of reading but involves active engagement with the interface and reflection on the game's rules and its behaviour, sometimes extending to the algorithms and codes that make the artefact work. It is here that technical reason informs cultural practice and becomes essential to contemporary aesthetics.

In his study of the first baroque, Walter Benjamin (1985) argued that its works were not important for their symbolic meaning-content. Indeed, if we read them at this level, their fascination for seventeenth-century audiences is perplexing, much as the appeal of computer games stands out as odd to reflective cultural critics who cannot find anything worthwhile in them.[10] In baroque works, the characters are undeveloped, the storylines are obvious and repetitive, and the audiences have to work too hard to extract anything worthwhile from them. Benjamin describes how the element of play and games becomes foregrounded in works of this era. This involved overt experimentation with dramatic convention, pushing the form of the play itself into the foreground and effectively trivializing themes that would once have carried heavy symbolic and religious meanings. He uses the example of death, a recurring theme in the baroque (and pivot of almost all computer game action), and describes how in baroque plays we find, "the replacement of the execution of the victim at the altar with his escape from the knife of the sacrificial priest; the destined victim . . . runs around the altar" (1985: 107). The goal of these works was not to project ideology but to overwhelm and inspire awe as well as laughter. Similarly, Maravall points out that in seventeenth-century Europe growing awareness of the power of mathematics went hand in hand with an enhanced place for "magic" symbols and an aesthetic of social space that drew heavily on them.[11] Pointing out that "all the very typical aspects of baroque culture relate to gaming" (1986: 192), Mara-vall argues that baroque culture was centrally concerned with converting magic symbolism into a dense web of visual entertainments that would guide the population by involving people actively, rather than by tradi-tional methods of issuing orders backed by coercive authority (1986: 68). The idea of a second, or neo-baroque, should prompt more critical detachment and suspicion because it signifies the political manipulation of culture. In this context, technical or instrumental reason becomes the bearer of a kind of cultural politics. Paradoxically, its aim seems to be the destruction of aesthetic properties, in the sense that there is a steadfast unwillingness to be suckered by the superficial, interface-level appear-ance of the story. However, it is the antagonism between the packaging and instrumental puzzle-solving play that *is* the aesthetic form of new media. Ultimately, much of the labour expended in unravelling these stories must be deemed wasted. Contemporary entertainment is aimed at creating distractions and overwhelming a confused and tired populace. However, at its heart is the tension between technology and aesthetics described by Fortunati. The player's activity is demystifying instrumental reason in pursuit of a meaning that only seems to be there in the game. The aesthetics of the computer game centre on this tension between play and its destruction of the illusions that make it possible. This points to a broader social logic of agency which has real political implications, some of which are explored in the next chapter.

Digital Technical Politics

7

Digital technology plays a central role in the modern, globalized economy. According to political economist Saskia Sassen (2006) most accounts of digital technology in relation to the economy remain fixed within a deterministic model, according to which computers "impact" upon economic and political processes.[1] She proposes to remedy this through a theory of cultures of interpretation. The centrality of information technology to any understanding of profound social changes of the last two decades should be seen as the result of specific social groups choosing to exploit its capabilities in ways that comport with their interests. My aim in this chapter is to bring this idea into conjunction with Feenberg's notion of progressive or democratic rationalization. The point of this is to develop the critical perspective on technology described in earlier chapters by applying it to current developments. At the same time, this move has reflexive implications for critical theory itself; in particular, it is an opportunity to break down the somewhat monolithic notion of a hegemonic technological rationality into something more nuanced and flexible.

The first section "Information and Power" examines one important attempt to comprehend information technologies in terms of a theory of power derived from Foucault. Mark Poster (1995, 2006) has argued that information technology is inherently progressive because it undermines the hegemony of modernist identities and creates openings for new subject positions. For him, the dynamics of modernist power are essentially spent in the digital era. Discussion of this leads into the second section "Hegemony and Web-Searching", which uses the example of web-searching and the rise of the Google search engine to illustrate design hegemony in Feenberg's sense. It will be recalled from the

135

discussion in Chapter 4 that, according to Feenberg the neutral appearance of technology is part of a political strategy of concealment. At the same time, it is an idea that is open to historical change, which is why Feenberg can avoid the accusation of substantivism. This example shows the ongoing relevance of modernist critical frameworks to digital technology and culture. The third section "The Digital-Global" examines Sassen's (2006) analysis of the use of networked computers by powerful social forces in the new economic order of globalization, which highlights how networked computer technology presents specific capabilities that are exploited by finance capital and other powerful social actors. That some capabilities are developed while others lie neglected is a central theme of her analysis and is consistent with the normative direction of the current work. Sassen argues that the new technology enters into a complex relationship with actors and social structures, especially frameworks of law, formed under the previous era of national industrial capitalism. Used in different ways by different social groups, technology reacts back on society, producing new social spaces; novel class formations and social logics that in turn drive subsequent developments, including further technological changes. In the fourth section "Beyond Technocracy?", I argue that Sassen's analysis enables us to deepen Feenberg's critical theory, differentiating the notion of technological rationality in a way that reflects the emergence of a new historical constellation. On this basis it is possible to reformulate Feenberg's technical politics as no longer a struggle against technocracy but instead as a conflict that includes a positive role for technical reason in the context of multiple social logics and shifting cultural horizons. The book concludes with some reflections on this, the redemption of technical reason in the digital era.

Information and Power

An influential account of the politics of digital technology is advanced by new media theorist Mark Poster. He sees the rise of a society based on information flows as holding out positive potential for social transformation. For him, information technology is an agent of postmodern social and cultural transformation that works towards the dissolution of "modernist tyrannies". Computers operationalize the radical critique of identity developed by post-structuralist thinkers, especially Foucault, in the 1960s and 1970s. Poster has developed a Foucauldian perspective on the database as the pre-eminent, or paradigmatic instance of a de-centred, diffuse form of social power that works by producing a proliferation of social subjects rather than through the generation of a regime of truth that people have to internalize. Emphasizing the constitutive role of discourse for human subjects, Poster notes a discrepancy between the impersonal character of many interactions between physical individuals and the intimate nature of the information that is routinely shared between inanimate databases. Buying something from a store, for instance, I may barely notice the sales assistant who swipes my card but as he does so he sets in train an extended dialogue between two or more databases. Information passes between them, involving all kinds of facts about me, my credit status and the consumer choices I am making. Other authors have noticed the ease with which these "data shadows" (Garfinkel 1999) can be manipulated in what has become known as "identity-theft". Acquiring information about someone from a database can become the basis for various "real world" crimes, which leave the affected person unable to obtain credit or, in the worst cases, implicated in crimes they did not commit. However, from Poster's perspective this new threat is not the sociologically salient factor that emerges from extensive commercial use of database and networked technology (1995).[2] Of greater significance is the new kind of subject that is produced by the interface of human individuals and complex, intelligent machines:

> Identity theft is a result of the new relation between humans and digital information machines, an interface that couples carbon-based and silicon-based beings in a new synergy. In the context of the human-computer interface, identity takes on a different configuration from the common-sense view that it is an interior state of consciousness, bounded by the skin of the individual.
>
> (2006: 92)

The significant change associated with informationalism is the proliferation of selves, all of them equally "real", that results. The "modernist illusion" that my sense of myself as located in that inner space just behind the eyes (Harre and Gillett 1994) corresponds to the real "me" is undermined by a proliferation of "mes", all of them equally real, hosted on databases and constituted through the dynamic interaction of intelligent software. The fact that I am unaware of these processes that they do not form a part of my conscious ratiocinations does not make them any less essential to who "I" am and what I do. A dispassionate analysis of a simple transaction in a store reveals that my natural body does very little, while an enormous amount of physical activity occurs at disparate places around the globe. For Poster, the pretence that what really matters is the self-conscious embodied element of the process, the attempt to privilege my consciousness in an account of the action of buying something, is little more than a humanist prejudice. There is a clear parallel between these views and those of Haraway and Latour, discussed in Chapter 5.

For Poster, though, information machines implement the post-structuralist assault on "modernist tyrannies of identity". As we saw in earlier chapters, capitalist modernity deployed discourses aimed at the normalization of subject populations. Having sexual orientations or impulses that contravened codes for normality could result in individuals being reprocessed so that they were re-invested with the appropriate understanding of themselves and then re-inserted into society having been "cured". Normalization meant being restored to a correct kind of unity with one's self, being an upright citizen with the right kinds of desires, maintaining a bourgeois public existence. In the new situation this disciplinary power, in which everyone keeps themselves under constant observation, gives way to a different kind of regime in which identity is fragmented, multiple and fluid. This, Poster argues, opens the way to more experimental approaches to self-hood in which we are not tied to bourgeois norms. Although subjects are still constrained by databases in the sense that they can do some things and not others – I can only buy so much in the store – the proliferation of selves means that more experimentation is possible. Virtual life and participation in cyber-culture enable us to assume other roles, without feeling tied to the identity attached to us by proximal, familiar social connections. We can join communities of people who share our interests and experience new kinds of freedom on this basis. A useful illustration of this might be the Burakumin people of Japan, who were an oppressed minority viewed as a kind of "unclean" cast by mainstream society (Gottlieb 2003). Using the Internet as a communications tool, Burakumin have established their own websites and, having acquired strength through association, have mounted successful challenges to their previous stigmatization in mainstream media. Burakumin identity has been challenged and renegotiated as a consequence of the new medium.

At the same time as it opens up possibilities like this for subject populations, the new technology reduces the powers of corporations and states to maintain traditional claims to authority. Information flows have made censorship much more difficult to maintain, for example, since information sensitive to one state may be freely available in another and Internet connections do not respect national boundaries. Similarly, software tools and products that only exist in the form of code cannot be guarded using traditional means – they are always open to being copied without injury to their original. Here properties integral to the new technology, in particular its seeming ability to transport messages around the world without impediment and its apparent lack of material substance, create an environment that is inherently problematic for the operation of modernist power. Poster envisages a new regime in which de-centred, multiple subjects play in openings provided for them by developing information infrastructure, and capitalist and government agencies struggle to maintain a form of control that no longer applies. However, this optimistic reading is curiously deterministic in its assessment of computer technology and incorporates fallacious assumptions about the intrinsic nature of computers and information itself (cf. Marx 2003).

Poster assumes throughout his work that information is unmediated or instantaneous. The fact that data travel down fibre optic cables at roughly the speed of light means that actions taken in one physical location are, in principle, also taken simultaneously at all other locations on a network. This underlies the virtual character of informational communications and it is an assertion that is replicated elsewhere in the literature on globalization and the "virtual economy". In contrast, Sassen (2006) acknowledges that informationalization modifies the spatio-temporal co-ordinates of specific economic entities. Since a fund or account may be registered in one territory and yet modified by and dependent upon actions performed upon it somewhere else, it becomes anomalous in a regulatory framework based on national territorial authority. However, she resists the hyperbole about virtuality, because for these entities to have any significance they must be, in Hayles's (1999) phrase, "instantiated in some material interface". Entities, like accounts and funds, are only entities for some person somewhere and they still hold a real place in the pragmatically delineated field of human affairs and social interactions. It is the role of interface design on information systems to filter and make useable data flows that would otherwise be redundant. One of the major contributions of Sassen's work has been to highlight the development of institutional regimes that reflect the needs of cultures of interpretation and the choices they have made in relation to when information stops flowing and gets parcelled up and incorporated into human affairs.

As we saw in the previous chapter, Poster accepts uncritically the notion that the standard for a "good" interface is that it should "disappear" or become transparent from the standpoint of the user. His analysis is fixated on the ontological character of information, whereas Sassen's charts emerging patterns of institutional control through regulation and changes in the nature of territorial sovereignty that develop in response to how information technology is actually used. Poster argues that its virtual and insubstantial character makes information inherently difficult to control and problematic for the authority of governments and corporations. Although there is some justification for this claim, writing to different media – the process of transferring data between material interfaces – continues to take time.[3] Moreover, unmediated data are just noise that interfaces filter and process to create information that can be interpreted and understood by a human user and these interfaces involve design decisions. Which data are screened out and defined as unwanted noise, as well as questions about the foregrounding of some kinds of information over others at the interface are all contingent on design decisions. To accept the dominant conception of interface design uncritically is to ignore key terrain in contemporary technical politics. Moreover, this terrain is being actively used by governments and powerful interest groups to steer and control subject populations, encouraging us to relate positively to some information while deterring us from using other sources. This politics of interface design and of filtering is a defining feature of the information age. While Poster presents his argument as a radical critique of modernity, his arguments actually end up supporting some of the most regressive tendencies in recent developments.

For example, his assertion that the mix of humans and machines "causes" identity theft, which is not unique to the cited comment, robs human agents of their responsibility for the actions that result in this state of affairs. Criminals and corporations who fail to make adequate checks before allowing data flows to occur are effectively exonerated as "assemblages", offloading their responsibility onto a cyborg infrastructure. The technology Poster describes in connection with store transactions has been designed with the interest of corporate retailers and banks in mind, rather than ordinary citizens. The burden of responsibility for verifying that I am who I say I am and that it is my own money I am spending has been put onto me, through the medium of the card. The card acts as a kind of interface between me and the world of global finance. Its rules are mainly set by the banks, and at the time of writing banks in the UK are attempting to deprive customers of the, until now, quite generous insurance safeguards concerning their use of cards, so that if we are deemed to be in any way "negligent" card users, customers and not the banks will suffer the losses. In Foucauldian terms this is the imposition of a new set of norms of subjectivity – you must become an adept and upright card user and not one of those lax people who lets their kids know their pin numbers – corresponding to a new discipline of citizenship. However, this reading is not available to Poster, who chooses to render such interfaces sociologically unproblematic.

Hegemony and Web-Searching

The standardization of public search engine technology over the last decade is an illustration of the fact that the merger of humans and informational machines is not so seamless a transition to a new regime of power as much contemporary theory suggests. We are often encouraged to believe that the World Wide Web and the Internet are inherently "open" arenas within which exploration and roaming free are the norm. However, the most common way of finding out where we want to go on the web is to use a search engine to guide us to sites containing material relevant to our interests. Particular search engines are popular and associated with a friendly and trustworthy experience of technology use. These things are especially true of Google, which has become the most popular search engine in the world over the last ten years (Economist 2006: 83–4). Google's success is partly attributable to the fact that it became well known its directory had achieved web coverage at around 15%.[4] Early search engines constructed their directories using a mixture of human (manual) editorial input and algorithms that counted the frequencies of terms within source pages linked to the net. These techniques generally achieved more limited coverage, because of the strains imposed by open-ended searching over an ever-growing system. Google introduced "spider bot" searching technology. Bots roam the web, choosing routes that are determined by a programmed algorithm, and build a directory of website addresses as they go. The technical distinctiveness of Google's bot has to do with its ability to count the number of links to a website from other sites, whose links are also counted. The result is that "By counting, weighting and calculating the link structures between web pages [Google's creators] . . . were able to return search results more relevant than those of any other search engine" (Economist 2006).

However, there has been a creeping standardization of publicly available web-searching techniques since the late 1990s, as other search engines have embraced Google style technology. A series of buy-outs during the first years of this century saw the effective elimination of rival technologies. The recent acquisition of Ask Jeeves by Teoma is one of the most recent examples of this tendency. Relatively new search engines, like Teoma or Surfwax, work by aggregating over the others, effectively assimilating data from other engines that are commonly running Google style bots, although there may be some variations in the precise algorithms they are using to guide the bots in their roving activities. The algorithms used to determine bot-behaviour are industry secrets and partly because their behaviour is not publicized, there is a race on among website creators, especially in the commercial sector, to manufacture websites that will fall in the path of search engine bots and seem to be well-connected when they do. This is called "positioning" and off-the-shelf software exists that employs knowledge of bot-behaviour to automate the positioning process itself. In this way, website designers and search engine companies are engaged in a curious tactical battle in which search engines strive to maintain their appeal to a wide user base by seeming to be efficient tools, while web-designers struggle to distort search engine behaviour in the pursuit of their commercial interests. The consequence of this is a remarkable uniformity of behaviour across all public search engines.

As Introna and Nissenbaum (2000) have argued, this means there is a politics of searching the web that has gone largely unreflected upon. Sites that are favoured by search engines enter the experience of many more users, defining a certain conception of what the web is and what it can be for most people. Relevance of content, especially towards the top of any given "list" is now ensured by counting the number of links to a site. Sites containing the searched for terms will be prioritized if they are linked to by many other sites and those other sites are themselves part of a dense web of interconnected sites. What matters here is what is excluded – the vast number of relevant websites that we do not see, especially on that all-important first page of search results. Lukes's definition of power applies to this case, since it is clear that while from the subjective point of view of actors using the technology it normally seems to work well an alternative set of circumstances would create better conditions for searchers and make for more open competition between website owners. A concern with what is left out of view in this way is, perhaps, all the more important when commercial interests increasingly shape search outcomes through "sponsored links", direct lobbying of human directory editors and the "positioning" activities of website designers discussed above. A preferable position would be to have more diverse search engine technology, running different algorithms. However, Google's popularity is explained in terms of its success. According to the Economist, "Google's share of searches has gone up almost every month of the past year", and "This is why people 'google' – rather than, say, 'yahoo' – their driving directions, dates and recipes" (Economist 2006: 83–4). Google is popular because it is popular and it is seen as the search tool of choice essentially because people believe that other people see it in those terms. But this standardization of a key filter for most web users in the information age must be seen as a powerful constraint on our use of the technology. This is perhaps best understood in terms of Feenberg's notion of a technologically implemented hegemony.

Reading current technology designs as if they were a political discourse, Feenberg hopes to establish grounds for a new critique of capitalist technocracy. The example of standardization in public searching tools might be taken as illustrative of his notion of a hegemonic technological rationality as a kind of horizon that limits innovation and arbitrarily restricts the scope of new designs. Far from over-turning modernist regimes of authority, digital technology design here works within a horizon that upholds capitalist values. As we saw in Chapter 4, a technical code condenses two levels of description associated with the technical object. One concerns the neutral functions or affordances it provides, while another "integrates" (2002: 179) the artefact into the dominant social logic. Once encoded, technical artefacts seem like neutral, technical solutions to practical problems and they present in this way to social actors who are looking for those kinds of objects. Codification ensures that the object now slots into a set of social arrangements in which it is formally biased in the sense discussed above. As more "problems" become subject to solution by codified objects in this sense, so we drift towards technocracy, in which discussion and democracy play a diminished role in the organization of social life. Viewed in this way, Google and other devices institutionalize the logic of the market – supply and demand – and suppress other principles that might be used to help effective searching.

The hegemonic technological rationality exerts a limiting or distorting effect on technology design. However, Feenberg argues that there is a technical politics located in the design of new technologies. His goal here is to incorporate some of the ideas of social constructionism into critical theory. The process of designing a new artefact involves social actors and groups and they bring to the table their own interests and practical investments in the new technology. As we saw in Chapter 2, this is the basic idea behind constructionism. However, constructionists have been criticized for failing to identify any political or historical context for their studies of specific technologies (Winner 1993). Feenberg proposes to remedy this by including the idea of a limiting cultural horizon that technology development and design processes always runs up against. Consequently, the struggles among relevant social groups take on a political dimension. When they compete for control over the final design of an artefact they compete for control of its technical codification and this has implications for the set of cultural values in the overall hegemonic technological rationality. Since technological rationality serves to define what technology is, progressive rationalization involves working within technology design to broaden the value horizon on technology development in the direction of a culture less dominated by capitalist values, especially narrow calculations of profitability. The situation is analogous to that in politics, where parties compete to make the electorate accept that their policies are most likely to lead to prosperity and fairness – very few politicians, and almost no successful ones, deliberately avoid associating their ideas with these things – each with the overall aim of pushing the social consensus towards greater consistency with their own preferred vision of social life.

There is politics, then, in the innovation process and one task of critical theory is to identify and encourage designs that might stretch the horizon set by hegemonic technological rationality in this way. In the case of search technologies, there are alternative tools on the web. For example, some people acquire and run their own search bots for around $50. These can be programmed to search according to a desired principle or principles and in this way the owner is able to build up their own directory of sites. There is little public information on what kind of social actor does this, but I would guess that it should be understood in the context of Eric Raymond's (1999) observation that most corporations do not use "off the shelf" software but prefer to produce it "in-house". Presumably customized bots are seen by some corporate players as a cost-efficient method for building their own knowledge of the web, which could perhaps be sold on but would be useful in itself for sourcing goods and services. There are also some attempts to experiment with the aesthetics of information retrieval, for example the search engines kartoo and ujiko.[5] These present the user with something more interesting than lists of links. Kartoo presents titles of webpages generated by the search in a map-like visual representation of the links that exist between relevant sites. There is also an interesting "drill down" facility which enables the user to add new terms to the search simply by moving the cursor around over the links. In this way, terms that describe the links are activated and entered into the search field. In terms of sites identified, however, these engines both exhibit high degrees of similarity to other search engines.

A third design alternative would be search engines whose directories are made by human editors. Increased use of bot technology to generate searchable directories has been associated with a reduced role for manual directory management. The best example of a search tool that retains human editors seems to be the "open directory" (http://dmoz.org/), which has been developed on an "open-source" basis[6] is edited by volunteer experts. It is an evolving database of points on the web that have been checked for the reliability of their content by knowledgeable people who are motivated to develop a useful and robust infrastructure for public web use. Unfortunately, perhaps due to the extensive role of humans in this work, the coverage of the open source directory is not estimated to be as high as commercial engines. The main consequence of this from the user's point of view is an increased number of null searches. Of the available alternatives this is probably the one that is most consistent with democratic rationalization. However, in an interesting recent development with potential there has been at least one attempt to link web-searching and the construction of directories to on-line community sites. *Stumbleupon.com* invites people to share their favourite websites by entering them on a database.[7] At the same time, they construct a profile of themselves that can be linked to by other users, but which also constitutes a filter when they use the directory. In much the same way that Amazon's website matches your previous purchases to items in its database and offers them to you, so this programme sits in your web browser and matches your browsing history and declared interests with items in the directory, drawing your attention to websites that people with similar profiles have entered. As the name implies, "stumbling" is a one-click game whose results are unpredictable – you are guided to a website that may (and usually does) comport with your interests – rather than a searching tool. Nonetheless, it does challenge the hegemonic technological rationality in the sense that it refuses the idea of web-searching as merely something we do for work or in a systematic, instrumental way and turns it into something more playful. *Stumbleupon.com* applies the community aspect of web use directly to searching and is effectively employing anyone who wants to play as a kind of editor, so it will be interesting to see how the project develops as the directory grows. As with all community websites there are issues concerning corporate management and the ownership and use of the data we enter, knowingly and inadvertently.[8]

The Digital-Global

Much of the literature on globalization explains the emergence of transnational corporations and of an increasing amount of economic activity that exceeds the regulatory boundaries of nation states with reference to networked computers (Castells 1996; Greider 1997; Gray 1998; Latham and Sassen 2005; Smith 2006). In her theory of globalization, Saskia Sassen (2006) argues that digital technologies have created a number of key capabilities which she sees as essential to the emergence of a new kind of global society in the current period (2006: 387). Networked computers introduce an unprecedented degree of interconnectivity between agents in disparate spatial locations; they enable multiple simultaneous transactions to occur between agents who are thusly dispersed and yet in contact, and in this way they create decentralized networks or assemblages that handle key social functions and practices. These capabilities are manifest in a range of extensions to and modifications of former operations in economy, politics and culture, which taken together demand a revision of our understanding of the distributions of power in and the mechanisms for that distribution in the modern world. Globalization on this view is not a straightforward phenomenon in which the nation state loses power and transnational bodies acquire it. On the contrary, in some respects the nation state actually gains certain functions and finds it has enhanced scope for action in specific domains. Digital technologies, though, have been used to create spaces for action and interaction that exceed the regulatory capacities of the nation state. A new set of economic processes and even entities have been created that, nonetheless, require, in Sassen's terminology, re-insertion into concrete social spaces, within the national. The result is a reconfiguration of the powers of the nation state itself, so that the executive function is enhanced, while the powers of elected assemblies tend to diminish, and surveillance intensifies while information flows become decentralized. The operation of social power is altered in the global-digital social formation.

These changes are not technologically determined, but reflect the outcomes of social choices and, in particular, of the meshing of novel technical infrastructures with prior cultures and practices. This sets in train a dialectic in which established social practices condition the reception of digital technologies and determine how they will be used, resulting in a changed situation in which the established social practices are themselves altered or assigned a different role in the new reality. In keeping with the argument of the current work, Sassen maintains that digital technologies hold out real possibilities but these have to be interpreted and to develop within prior cultures and practices. She also recognizes that technology designs necessarily result in the neglect of some possibilities even as they promote others (2006: 341). This opens the door to the critical method advocated here of seeking implied counterfactuals with which to contrast current social situations and on which basis normative assessments can be made of the social significance of technology. It is also the context for a differentiated picture of the social interests that are shaping networked digital technology:

> ... the actors shaping the development of the Internet diverge sharply, ranging from the original group of computer scientists that developed the open and decentralised features of the Internet to multinational corporations concerned with intellectual property rights protection. Most recently there has been a strengthening of civic and political groups concerned with the extent to which private separate interests are shaping Internet access and development.
>
> (Sassen 2006: 331)

In previous chapters, I have indicated that the personal computer was shaped in its development by a combination of occasionally contradictory social forces. The most recent phases of this social shaping were informed by the development of networking technology, which involves a range of techniques that enable computers to exchange information.

Initially, the Internet excited commentators and users alike because it was experienced as the opening up of a new kind of space, alongside the so-called real world, within which people could experience new freedoms. Early reflection on this experience associated "virtual space" with a liberating disembodiment. In cyber-space it would be possible to establish an alternative society, even to create a virtual utopia freed from material constraints (Rheingold 2000; Turner 2006). However, the main driver of innovation in the social employment of networked digital computers has not been utopia but the world of global financial markets. Moreover, digital technology does not involve an escape from material constraints or the reality that this is a physical universe. As Sassen points out, digitization is "merely a different type of materiality" (2006: 344). It presupposes fixed infrastructure, computers and phone lines, while its seemingly unstoppable mobility is actually contained within about forty of what she calls "global cities" (2006: 315) where this infrastructure is particularly well developed.

Sassen identifies four new social classes associated with the digital-global social formation (cf. Lash 2002: 29). These are the new class of experts, who understand the technological infrastructure; bureaucrats and officials, who have technical expertise pertaining to regulatory frameworks and other varieties of social engineering; hacktivists, who are oppositional sub-groups that include individuals with technical knowledge; and the poor, especially migrant groups (2006: 298). These global classes do not exist in "cyber-space" and they are not "cosmopolitan" in outlook. Globalization sees them each bring their own distinctive set of interests to the shaping of technology and technologically constituted environments. In Feenberg's terms, they are each concerned with enlarging their operational autonomy (2002: 76) through engagement with the technology, but this leads them to pursue quite different, even conflicting strategies:

> Each remains embedded, in often unexpected ways, in thick, localised environments. The localised microstructures of daily civic life and struggles, and the translocal insertions of immigrants. And each of these classes is guided by a single logic rather than the multiple logics at the heart of genuine cosmopolitanism: profits in the case of the new professional elites (no matter how cosmopolitan their tastes for, say, culture); specific and narrow governance issues in the case of government networks; and specific local struggles and conflicts in the case of global civil society, diasporas and immigrant networks. (2006: 300)

This vision of competing social groups, each with their own investments in the technology and each trying to impose their vision of a future in which they have more freedom (see also Thrift 2006), sits very easily with Feenberg's notion of technical politics as a contest for hegemony within technology design. The determination of technology development is not limited to software on computer networks, but extends to other innovations within digital technology. In 2006, for example, new methods of secure financial transfer using mobile phones were developed, specifically to facilitate migrant workers who want to send money home from the rich countries to their families in the global South (Economist 2007).

Contemporary technology development is running along four distinct trajectories, corresponding to the interests of the four most dynamic sections of the contemporary social world. Each is associated with what Sassen calls different "substantive social rationalities", corresponding to the social classes and their pursuit of their interests through digital technical systems, as well as to the changed institutional landscape and especially the new distributions of power associated with globalization. The first and in many ways most important shaping interest has been that of the global finance capital markets:

> While digitisation of instruments and markets was critical to the sharp growth of the global capital market and thereby enabled the financialising of economic criteria, this outcome was shaped by interests and logics that typically had little to do with digitisation per se, even though it was crucial. The logic of use at work is not that of the technology as such but of finance, one to be distinguished no matter how important these technologies have been for its growth and character.
>
> (2006: 337)

As early as the 1980s, finance capitalists with programming skills and mathematical expertise began using digital technologies to fabricate financial products. The consequence has been a proliferation of investment tools and methods that presuppose entities whose existence is fundamentally mathematical and generated in the "virtual"[9] space of networked computers. The main example of this is derivatives markets, where investors essentially shape the mathematics of risk assessments within the global marketplace. These operations are made possible through a process known as softwaring (2006: 351). Sassen describes the impetus towards such activity in the following terms, which bring out its character as a substantive social logic driven by the interest a particular social stratum has in profit:

> ...a crucial incentive for innovation is the push to liquefy forms of wealth hitherto considered non-liquid. This can require enormously complex financial instruments and has driven much innovation. The possibility of

using computers has not only facilitated the widespread use of these instruments but has also enabled the widespread use of these instruments insofar
as much of the complexity can be contained within the software. Use does
not require full understanding of the financial mathematics or the software
algorithms involved.

(2006: 254)

This use of digital technology clearly has profound implications for the
regulatory powers of the nation state, since capital is now mobile in a
completely new way (cf. Leyshon *et al.* 2003). It also affects people whose
economic means of subsistence may be devastated by the removal of
factories or other means of employment. Consequently, globalization is
also associated with new conflicts and waves of migration as people try
to reach one of the nodal points in the new networked economy and to
avoid being trapped in one of the emerging points of anarchy within the
global state system (cf. Castells 1996); places where their only prospects
involve humiliation (Smith 2006) and worse.

Migrants and the resource-poor within the wealthy countries form the
locus of another social rationality that acts to shape digital networks. As
Sassen puts it, "power, contestation, inequality and hierarchy inscribe
electronic space and shape the criteria for what types of software get
developed" (2006: 341). These socially marginal groups who use computer
networks to maintain connections constitute the emergence of new kinds
of articulation of subjective experience to broader social movements,
which Tim Jordan (2002) groups under the heading of "hacktivism".
Hence, migrants maintain connections with groups in their "home"
countries; environmentalists living in large cities can communicate with
people elsewhere in the world who are seeing directly the effects of
deforestation and so on. These novel social networks also drive the development of alternative software technologies, such as the free web browser
program Mozilla firefox, or Skype, the program that allows people to
make free phone calls on the web. Recently, a group of hackers created a
program to protect firefox users from being traced by regulatory agencies,
or anyone else (Spacewar 2006). This drive to use digital technology to
establish new communications networks is related to a third substantive
social logic, not singled out by Sassen but important to my argument.
Hackers and technology enthusiasts enjoy digital technology for its own
sake. For them it is a source of pleasure in itself and the outcome of
their activity is innovation, some of it redundant, some taken up and
used by other social agents. Shareware programs and the open source
movement make software freely available to people who often would be
unable to afford off-the-shelf versions, for example. These developments
constitute an alternative social logic shaping the digital realm, although

they are clearly less powerful than global capital. That the latter enjoy greater success in shaping digital technology to their interests can be seen from the fact that the great majority of new software produced in the last decade has been related to firewalls and security, much of it related to the stand-off between the computer security industry and those labelled as hackers (Taylor 1999). The impact of the kind of exploratory, in some ways purposeless attitude, which is characteristic of this group, is not always beneficial. In part, it encourages the increased and increasing emphasis on what Sassen calls "cyber-segmentation" – the construction of zones within digital networks that are not designed to be accessed by everyone equally. This zoning of computer networks was always a feature of computer network infrastructure but is currently growing in significance.

A fourth logic that emerges in this context is that of a new international regime of surveillance. As the nation state loses many of its traditional functions to the private, corporate sector and the role of democratic fora in checking the behaviour of states diminishes, the executive arm of the state gathers more powers to spy on its citizens and a new impetus to develop integrated information on citizens at the supranational level. Recent disputes between the European Union and US authorities concerning information on air travellers should be seen in this context, as should the recent proposal for an EU-wide biometrics database (Espiner 2005). Sassen characterizes the expanded secrecy of the state, alongside reduced privacy for private citizens as "part of the epochal transformation of the current age" (2006: 410). This function of the state is made possible by propensities of digital technology. When fingerprinting was invented in the nineteenth century, elements within the French state had the idea that it would be desirable to fingerprint the entire population. The idea, however, turned out to be impractical. Having millions of card files with fingerprints on would have rendered each individual record useless because of the time it would take to search through them all looking for a match for one found at a crime scene. As Simpson Garfinkel (1999) points out, this is what changes with the use of digital computers to create searchable databases. Digital technology facilitates automated, near-instantaneous searching of databases that can contain detailed information on populations of several countries. The richness of these data when combined in huge databases is a factor that should give us pause for thought. In a recent study of mobile phone data, Green and Smith (2004) show how telephone companies have the power to build up a record of user activities that far exceeds monitoring of movement. Data on geographic location combine with other pattern of user information and correlate with those of other users who receive texts and calls. Triangulated with other information, that grows richer as mobiles become more multi-functional, the result is not merely "indexical" but "iconic". The company know your movements, but they also know what kind of person you are. The contemporary state, confronted with increasingly mobile populations and a reduction in its effectiveness as far as other strategies of social control are concerned is motivated to devise ever more sophisticated methods for monitoring the behaviour of global citizens. Another recent example of this tendency driving the design of technical artefacts emerged recently when activist-researchers at the Electronic Frontier Foundation (EFF) discovered that dots produced by laser printers contained tiny code that would enable the US government to identify the source of any document printed using them. The dots are less than one millimetre in diameter, and they encode the date, time of printing and serial number of the printer. A spokesperson for the EFF said that the discovery,

> ... shows how the government and private industry make backroom deals to weaken our privacy by compromising everyday equipment like printers. The logical next question is: what other deals have been made to ensure that our technology rats on us?
>
> (Spacewar 2005)

This drive towards more powerful surveillance constitutes a fourth substantive social logic that is actively shaping digital technology. The meaning of technology and technological rationality for all these social actors has changed in the post-industrial, digital era, consequent upon these developments.

Beyond Technocracy?

Since the 1960s, critical theory of technology has concentrated its fire on the idea of technocracy. In essence, this critique has alleged that modern societies have allowed an increasing number of their operations to be taken over, if not by actual technologies then by agencies charged with providing solutions that are defined technically, as an alternative to those that are reached deliberatively. In this way democracy and civil society have been undermined in their capacity to steer society towards forms of life that have been chosen for their intrinsic desirability. This tendency is understood by Habermas in terms of "colonisation", in which a technical attitude that is quite legitimate in its own sphere of operations spills over into domains of life that ought to be structured around communication. Marcuse understood it as built into the character of modern technology, fulfilling its Heideggerian destiny. The most nuanced version of the technocracy thesis is probably Feenberg's argument that technical solutions appear as irresistible because of the hegemonic technological rationality that is coded into them during the design process. The technical code condenses technical principles aimed at achieving a specified end with social objectives and values that comport with the needs of capital. However, the processes described above require us to reflect on whether technocracy is still a useful diagnostic device applied to modern societies. The change to a digital or informational society and culture creates problems for the argument in all three of its main dimensions: The notion of a monolithic hegemonic technological rationality seems to be undermined; the question of aesthetics in technology design is posed in a radically new form, and the negative, or at best ambivalent, portrayal of instrumental or technical reason in critical theory seems out of step with contemporary political reality. In conclusion, I will try to assess how current tendencies impact upon critical thinking about technology with reference to each of these aspects.

The hegemonic technological rationality of the present includes a broader set of values than efficiency defined in terms of crude measures of profit and loss. It now accommodates the demand for elegant designs that are pleasing to use. This aesthetic imperative is an essential part of the codification of any new digital artefact. Beneath the surface of these designs are the demands for interfaces that perpetuate and amplify differential distributions of knowledge and, related to this, for enhancements to police and surveillance functions in new artefacts. The interconnectedness of digital technologies means that even if these functions are not present in designs when they come to market, powerful agencies will normally seek them out and exploit them. At the same time, other social forces will try to resist this, as we saw above. What underscores these developments is the essential openness of digital technological artefacts. They rarely come thoroughly encoded as technical in Feenberg's sense of representing a finished and obvious solution to a problem. When they are put forward in this way, there is invariably someone somewhere who undermines the established design and produces something that other people want to use. Manipulating technical objects in this way, to get them to do something other than what their designer intended is the original meaning of the term "hack". All digital artefacts are prone to hacking and all interfaces are informed at some level by the drive to prevent this and to control how the objects are used. In one obvious sense, the dynamics of this are consistent with Feenberg's idea of a technical politics. However, the form it currently takes does not normally involve the imposition of a dull, technical design with an interface that communicates the necessity of compliance by association with ideas of efficiency and good sense, resisted by users seeking to broaden the definition of efficiency. Rather, the interface will tend to be aesthetic and seductive and aimed at inhibiting the user from dabbling and experimenting with technical levels within the artefact. The technical politics of digital artefacts involves authoritative designs projecting the ideal of comfortable and enjoyable use, while those who resist are less concerned with this. In a sense, power is more duplicitous, since it conceals its operations beneath an aesthetic veneer, but at the same time it is obliged to be more open in the sense that values are explicitly formulated in the design of digital artefacts. Neither aspect conforms to the attempt to secure control of a technical code, characteristic of hegemonic technological rationality. Design conflicts now are more like arguments in which contrary or opposed statements are made through the medium of material artefacts themselves.

Hegemonic technological rationality was important in a context where the central social antagonism was that between labour and capital. For Feenberg, for example, the central opposition is the traditional one of self-realization through labour and cultural expression versus domination under the rubric of efficiency. However, as Sassen's analysis shows, in the contemporary global economy there are *multiple* social logics at work shaping digital technology. While the issue of control remains central it is best understood in terms of the drive to control risks posed by technological complexity, under conditions where there is increased demand from the populace for openness in technical systems. Sometimes these risks are centred on technology itself, as is the case with computer hackers. When hackers trespass into networks and systems they often do not know what consequences their actions will have and, although these are often exaggerated in the popular media, there is legitimate concern about this. At the same time, hackers are iconic rebels of digital culture because most people sense that their own use of computer and other resources is being arbitrarily scrutinized and on occasion even impeded not in the interests of safety but because they are being manipulated into buying something, or distracted from their own goals in a situation. The central contradiction of digital-global society seems not to be that between capitalist efficiency and workers' self-realization but rather between risk-management through surveillance as against openness in technology design and innovative use of technology as a locus of free creativity and enhanced efficiency. In this changed context, hegemony remains a useful concept to apply to technology designs, but it no longer seems to work by foisting technical or instrumental rationality onto subject populations. Instead, it tends to be more open to interpretation and variously encoded, corresponding to the variety of social contexts into which it is being projected. Rather than a singular technological rationality at work there are a range of substantive social rationalities actively shaping digital technology in accordance with specific hegemonic projects, linked to particular sub-cultures of interpretation. This subverts the idea of a mono-lithic technological rationality that controls all technology design within a narrow capitalist horizon.

Under contemporary design standards, digital artefacts are more likely to be assessed on their ability to insinuate themselves into our collective practices by way of their communicative powers and their aesthetics. Objects are assessed for their usability, their consistency with current meaningful practices, rather than their ability to perform narrowly defined functions. Success for a given design is not guaranteed by an appearance of being a machine or a technical object but rather tends to be a matter of how well the artefact signifies its functionality signs at its interface. Pointing a mouse and clicking an icon *is* the action of launching a web browser; pressing "return" is the same thing as initi-ating a task and these things are assured by meaningful images and words on the screen or spoken by a voice synthesizer. Technology is not closed and thereby commensurate with capitalist economic values. Instead, it is communicative and its association with human purposes is secured through messages sent using aesthetic and textual means and received by human users who are culturally equipped, rather than tech-nically trained, to interpret them. However, while Poster would have us believe that this supplants the idea of a critical reading of modern tech-nologies, it means that a political space opens up behind the machine's interface. Whether the design really is the best method; whether the programme does something we want doing or is actually a retrograde development; whether it conceals neglected possibilities, are all questions that are blocked not by the hegemony of technological rationality but by a range of context-specific communicative and aesthetic strategies. To unpack them requires a new articulation of technical expertise to crit-ical agency and this is what we see in the form of hackers and other non-formalized layers of expertise within digital-global culture. Sassen says that technical standards in this context work directly as "instruments of public policy" (2006: 335). In Feenberg's terminology, the technical code becomes explicitly meaningful with digital objects and it ceases to feign neutrality as the embodiment of pseudo-natural necessity. This is related to the new aesthetics of technology, discussed in the previous chapter. The aesthetics of the human–technology interface takes on a new significance in the design of digital artefacts and there is an enhanced role for meaning-oriented interpretation. Since capitalism remains the basis for economic life, this re-aestheticization of technology is problem-atic for Feenberg's analysis. According to his theory, technology should become more aesthetic and feel more "natural" only as part of a move away from the technological horizon imposed by that system. What this development highlights is the neutrality of technical reason, in particular, the fact that it is not implicated in capitalist violence. For Feenberg re-aestheticization was necessary for progressive technical politics because capitalism gave technical reason free reign over society, culture and nature and this had to be countered. Whereas pre-capitalist technology was encased in a cultural container or shell, and this prevented the originary violence of the technological relation from spilling over, capitalist societies removed this constraint on technical reason, with the result that people treated nature, other people and themselves as objects to be worked on. However, the idea of cultural containment of technology feels redundant in the current context because culture – the realm of meaning – is being deployed through interface design as part of a strategy of containing technical reason, which is frequently allied not with global capital but with movements aimed at enhancing human freedom – through communication, but also through technical experimentation itself.

The activities of computer hackers, open source programmers and the creators of shareware are all heavily informed by technical reason. There is little evidence from the way they discuss their work of them investing it with any ideological significance over and beyond the intrinsic value of making technology work better and in a way that is more free from social influence, for good or ill. An interesting early example of the idea that this kind of fixation on technical detail constitutes resistance without ever making an explicit appeal to ideologies was provided by the "considents" in the Soviet Union in the 1950s and 1960s. Cybernetics was developed in the Soviet Union by a small group of a few hundred computer scientists. Like their Western counterparts, they were interested in developing computers and robots to automate processes that humans found onerous. However, they also resembled their Western peers in seeing progressive social function for their work. Just as Norbert Weiner tried to contact the labour unions to alert them to the dangers of automation (Noble 1984), so Soviet cyberneticians envisaged their systems taking over the command and control function of the Soviet bureaucrats and time-servers. According to Gerovitch (2000), they dissented from the official goal of using computers to enhance party control of society and management control of the workplace, not on the basis of a liberal critique of Soviet society but because they thought computers could be used to implement socialism. They understood socialism as the rational organization of production and distribution, not in terms of the slogans of Soviet ideology. As such, the considents (consenting dissidents) were the first geek critics of society and their critique was built into the systems they designed, in the detail. The considents embodied technical reason and to some extent would have fit the definition of technocrat. However, they tried to resolve the tension between their aspirations and technological rationality in the direction of a closer affiliation with the technology itself and a reduction of meaning-investments in the machine. They point the way towards hacktivists (Jordan 2002), who are aware of possibilities in technology and negotiate them through engagement with its detailed structure.

Contemporary technical politics involves a detachment of technical rationality from its long-established association with social power. The computer interface sees aesthetics in design being used to reinforce social power relations, while more challenging designs that require people to engage in technical reason tend to be associated with a more liberated and expressive use of computer technology. In this way, computer technology is both shaped by and implicated in the changed configuration of the communicative, technical and economic dimensions of social life in digital society. Technical reason redeems itself while, as we saw in Chapter 6, "artistic" or aesthetic values become tools of capitalist cultural domination. Technology now includes the idea of "fun", yet it is no closer to liberating most people on the planet from what Karl Marx called the "heteronomy of need" (1981).

These epoch-defining changes associated with digital technology changes do not mean that we should collapse the distinctions essential to critical thought. Rather, the idea of a hegemonic power that employs strategies of concealment to reproduce the advantages of specific social groups should be brought back in to comprehend the new degree of and role for reflexivity in technology design. Technological rationality is contested and shaped by agents and groups with different power allocations. There is what Latour and others call a "micro-politics" that centres on specific artefacts and involves disputes over what they are for, how they ought to be used and the reasons for these judgements. Whereas traditional critical theory opposed communication and cultural value to technocracy, the new situation sees technical reason redeeming itself in the struggle to create open technical systems that test the limits of power in its control over technology design and over the kinds of values our culture invests in technology generally.

The ultimate goal of traditional critical theory was self-realization, achieved through a conquest of the labour process itself. In Marx's famous phrase, when socialism happens labour will cease to be the source of drudgery in life and become "life's prime want". However, not all technology designs are problematic; we need to discriminate between designs that are consistent with the goals of democracy, participation and freedom for individuals to develop fully and those that suppress or distort information in ways that tend to menace those values. This involves assessing technology – here interfaces on digital artefacts and specific configurations of functionality – in social context. Often, as Lukes's theory suggests, power works at levels that are not thematized explicitly in public discourse and it is the function of critique to draw these out. In the current period, novel social logics have moved to the fore and are shaping digital technology. These logics are not monolithic and the outcomes of the current mesh of technology with social relations are more subject to willed, politically inspired influence than has been the case in previous periods of human history.

Notes

1 Technology and Social Power

1. It is widely acknowledged, for example, that the Betamax video system was at least as efficient as VHS, while the case of the environmentally efficient electric car that was wilfully suppressed by manufacturers in the 1990s has been the subject of a hit movie (Paine, C. 2006). Fourteenth-century China constructed a fleet of ships that would have dwarfed those that left Europe a hundred years later but had them destroyed (Levathes 1994). Destructive techniques include the fairly widespread use, in the 1920s, of radium and related compounds to cure headaches and other minor complaints, resulting in horrible death (See Science Museum of Minnesota 2006).

2 The Meaning of Technology

1. Hermeneutics is a sub-discipline of philosophy that tries to understand how it is that we interpret meanings, or extract the content of messages. The root of the term is *hermes*, the name of the Greek messenger God (Mueller-Vollmer 1994: 1).
2. Bijker writes that once the technological frame becomes established "not everything is possible any more" (1997: 192), but of course everything was never possible.
3. In one of the founding texts of constructionism, David Bloor (1976: 12) acknowledges that people everywhere reason in much the same way but denies this has anything to do with a basic orientation towards the truth that is shared across cultures.
4. Davidson defines supervenience as follows: "a predicate p is supervenient on a set of predicates S if and only if p does not distinguish any entities that cannot be distinguished by S" (2005b: 187).
5. For authors in the constructionist discipline of Science and Technology Studies (STS), questioning the role of truth in explaining the success of science is almost a methodological first principle; see Sismondo (2004) and Bauchspies *et al.* (2006). There is, as Boghossian (2006) has pointed out, a gulf between contemporary philosophy and social theory on this issue.

6. At this point it is interesting to note that in a discussion of Bijker's book, the bicycle historian Nick Clayton has suggested that Bijker and his constructionist allies greatly exaggerate the role of social factors and social meanings invested in the artefact in their account of the shaping of the early bicycles (Clayton 2002; see also Epperson 2002). In fact, he argues, it was obvious to all parties to this dispute that once pneumatic tyres arrived on the scene, various qualities quite obviously desirable in a bicycle were going to eliminate the large front-wheeled variety.

7. Other examples of technologies with similar or identical purposes springing up in diverse historical and cultural locations include printing presses, water wheels, paddle boats and spinning wheels (see Pacey 1999).

8. The changes made incorporated Copernican mathematics into the Catholic calendar, even though Copernicus's thesis of helio-centric motion, essential to the validity of his results, was later condemned as blasphemous.

3 Modernity Theory

1. As pragmatist philosopher C.S. Peirce argued, "everybody", regardless of culture or place in history, "uses the scientific method about a great many things and only ceases to use it when he does not know how to apply it" (1998: 133).

2. For useful discussions of the idea of progress, see Bock (1978) and Bury (1920).

3. See, for example, Marx (1982: 42), where he writes that the starting point for any history must be human individuals and their physical relationship to the environment and their "modification in the course of history through the action of men".

4. Watt invented the engine in 1755 and, according to Hobsbawm (1999: 25) it was widely used in industry by 1769.

5. It is important to note here that science and scientific discoveries as well as not being peculiarly European were also not important to the new technologies of the nineteenth century. Indeed, many capitalists saw science as irrelevant to their activities, while the inventions of Watt, Cort and others seem to have owed little to abstract scientific knowledge. There were conflicts within the bourgeoisie concerning the relative importance of science and technology until the 1890s. Unlike science, technology did not challenge Christianity, the preferred ideology of most British capitalists in the nineteenth century (Gieryn 1999).

6. "Where there was textile manufacture, there were work bells." (Landes 1983: 73).

7. There is a residue of Marx's ambivalence here, since Adorno and Horkheimer endorse the idea of technical progress in the minimal sense that through its agency humanity "grows up": "Against the will of its leaders, technology has changed human beings from children into persons" (1979: 155).

8. Hence, Turgot could write in 1749 that, "Mathematical truths, becoming from day to day more numerous and hence more fruitful, point the way to the development of hypotheses which are more far-reaching and more precise, and indicate new experiments which, in their turn, present new problems for mathematics to resolve. Thus the need perfects the tool; thus mathematics is sustained by natural philosophy, upon which it sheds its light; thus everything is bound together; thus, in spite of the diversity in their development, all the sciences render mutual aid to one another..." in Meek (1973: 46).

9. Twentieth-century machine tool makers also customized their tools in this way (Noble 1984).

10. He explicitly identifies primary instrumentalization with Heidegger's technological mode of revealing and with Adorno's critique (2002: 175–6).

11. I am grateful to John Wilson for this example.

12. This aspect of Feenberg's theory is discussed by Stump (2000) and Thomson (2000a,b).

4 Social Domination

1. Feenberg cites part of this passage and mistakenly suggests that Marx attributes this role to science rather than machinery (2002: 48).

2. Some Marxists assert that the integrity of labour relates to its ontological status, in other words it stands prior to craft or other historical articulations each of which would be subject to its own critique. This view is expressed most clearly in Arthur (2002) and Meikle (1985).

3. Labour unions in the US and elsewhere did protest against the ways in which automation was implemented in the 1970s and 1980s, but there was never a mass movement against automation or a concerted attempt to save more than a percentage of the jobs lost; see Noble (1984).

4. Noble (1984: 71) goes so far as to align specific approaches within mathematics and science with attitudes towards social and political issues, contrasting the conservative computer scientist, John von Neumann with the liberal founder of cybernetics, Norbert Weiner.

5. Noble points out that robotics continued to use R/P techniques until the 1980s, but he does not explore the reasons why it was given up then.

6. Braverman is paradoxical on this point: "Considered only in their physical aspect, machines are nothing but developed instruments of production

whereby humankind increases the effectiveness of its labour . . . But within the framework of capitalist social relations, all this is reversed. The means of production become the property of the capitalist, and the past as dead labour takes the form of capital. The purely physical relationship takes the form given to it by capitalism and itself begins to be altered . . . capitalism . . . brings into being this system of the domination of the living by dead labour not just as an allegorical expression . . . but as a *physical fact*." (1974: 227–8).

7. Something seriously contemplated by Sherry Turkle (1995: 61).

8. A move initiated by Laclau and Mouffe (1985).

9. Commonly the interpretation of technology is limited to assessing how we use an artefact correctly to achieve an objective. It tends to be thought of as meaningless because its use becomes habitual. Hence, for Habermas, it becomes "second nature" and falls below the radar of hermeneutics.

10. Including James Watt's design for a steam-powered "rotative couch", or "human centrifuge" that would spin the patient in a special bed attached to a vertical column. The shock of being spun was said to have beneficial effects (Paine, S. 2006).

11. Something similar is attempted by Mark Poster (1995).

12. In his development of a post-structuralist theory of hegemony in connection with information technology, Mark Poster acknowledges the need for such limits but is unable to specify any criteria for setting them (1995: 42).

5 The Limits of Social Constructionism

1. In a similar vein, Habermas argues that institutions in the systems sphere, including technology, become reified into a kind of "second nature" (1995).

2. In Poland, for instance, state-owned enterprises manufactured the Meritum and UniPolBrit computers (Kirkpatrick 2007).

3. I am grateful to Tom Lean for allowing me to consult his (2004) Master's dissertation for information on the Spectrum and to James Sumner for sharing some of his detailed understanding of this period in the history of computing.

4. For early reservations, within computer science, concerning the benefits of more interactive systems, see Fitter (1979) and Nickerson (1976). Turkle goes on to say that, "for now, many are unwilling to accept the computer as an entity whose structure can be safely ignored".

5. An early pioneer here was Shulamith Firestone (1984) who, among other things, envisaged a technological future in which women would be relieved of the burdens of childbearing by mechanical wombs.

6. Hayles puts this as follows: "No longer is human will seen as the source from which emanates the mastery necessary to dominate and control the

environment" (1999: 290), although she retains the progressive political ideal of an autonomous subject who is not instrumental in this sense.

7. MOO is an acronym for "Multi-player Object-Oriented", which describes the kind of programme that the game is – essentially, a large database populated by interactive programmable objects. The Greek letter Lambda denotes the version of the programme. Players control characters who are themselves programmed objects, meaning that they have specific capabilities within the database. The game presents to players as a text description of a large house with an enormous subterranean basement. Players steer their characters around LambdaMOO by typing in text commands for movement and communicate with other players by entering the command for "speak" and following it with their intended utterance.

8. Gershenfeld argues that the open source movement, in which programmes are written and made available for free (see n. 6 in Chapter 7 for a fuller definition) is a good model in this area. If this were followed the result would be a library of instructions for the production of items, which users could download and use to make the objects, as long as they had the requisite raw materials.

9. For a representative sample of others working in this field, see Law and Hassard (1999).

10. For related discussion, see Kirsch and Mitchell (2004).

11. "...: no one knows how many people are simultaneously at work in any given individual; conversely, no one knows how much individuality there can be in a cloud of data points" (Latour 2005: 54).

12. Anyone who thought that ANT was motivated by a desire to secure recognition at the level of social reflection for the behavioural complexity of contemporary artefacts will be corrected by Latour's comment above on the *dysfunctional* computer as mediator.

6 Technology as Culture

1. See also Crary (1993) on the cultural twists and turns affecting the visual sense in the modern era.

2. Game modders are gamers who re-programme existing games. The resulting programmes are called mods (modifications) and often made available over the web. Some mods have become successful commercial games in their own right, the most famous example being "Counter-Strike" (1999), which was a modification of the game "Half-Life" (Valve 1998).

3. Software that makes heavy use of pictures and electronic trinkets is also less accessible to computers in countries with poorer infrastructure (Sassen 2006: 367).

4. Vertov argued his cinema was "A revolution in seeing, and therefore in man's reception of the world in general. A free, which means an active, conception of even the most mundane things" (Tsivian 2004: 84).
5. Stallabrass (1996) is similarly disparaging.
6. Melucci (1996) argues very plausibly that it is also culturally resurgent in the digital era.
7. I am suggesting that virtuality works here for some computer game scholars in the way that, for film theorist Andre Bazin the development of cinema was guided by the myth of "an integral realism, a recreation of the world in its own image". (Bazin 1967: 21)
8. Focillon (1992) argues that forms recur in times and places that may be very distant through a quasi-biological process he calls mitosis. This process connects patterns found in the art of disparate cultures.
9. It is because games are like this that many parents are simply unaware of their contents, since opening sequences and screens often contain no clues (cf. Funk 2001).
10. Mark Poster (1995) repeatedly derides games as "violent" and "masculine".
11. Eisenstein points out that print, the medium of enlightenment itself, was also used to produce texts filled with "baroque decoration" and mystical symbols. The medium was used to encourage "new forms of mystification" as well as to disseminate learning (1983: 43).

7 Digital Technical Politics

1. A tendency in sociological writing about computers that was criticized more than ten years ago by Edwards (1995).
2. To be fair, having played down the seriousness of identity theft in earlier works, Poster does acknowledge that the problem is "far from trivial" in his latest work (2006: 94).
3. For further discussion of related issues, see Ratto (2005).
4. See Searchenginewatch.com for more details.
5. These can be accessed at http://www.kartoo.com/ and http://www.ujiko.com/, respectively.
6. "Open source" designates a model of computer practice whereby programmes are written by groups of people in collaboration with new iterations circulated on the web and improved upon. The programmes are normally made available free, or under a "creative commons" license, which allows subsequent users to contribute to the process of improvement. The classic illustration of this process has been the Linux-operating system, invented by Finnish programmer Linus Torvalds and developed by him and the hacker community (see Moody 2002).

7. I am indebted to Theodor Araby-Kirkpatrick for bringing this to my attention.
8. One of the largest community websites is Face Book, which started as a way for people in the US education system to develop friendship networks. Membership entails signing an agreement that the owners of the site may sell your details on to third parties, although they deny ever having done this (Wikipedia 2007).
9. It is important to notice that in this context "virtual" denotes a space that is problematic from the perspective of regulation by established bodies like nation states. It signifies the dislocation of territorial sovereignty associated with globalization and has only a rhetorical connection with the aesthetic ideas discussed in Chapter 6. The fact that the term occurs in both contexts, although with very different meanings, is indicative of its role in contemporary hegemonies.

References

Adas, M. (1989) *Machines as the Measure of Man: Science, Technology and Ideologies of Western Dominance* London: Cornell University Press.

Adorno, T.W. (1973) *Negative Dialectics* London: RKP.

Adorno, T.W. (1986) *The Jargon of Authenticity* London: RKP.

Adorno, T.W. (2002) *Aesthetic Theory* London: Continuum.

Adorno, T.W., Horkheimer, M. (1979) *Dialectic of Enlightenment* London: Verso.

Anderson, B. (1983) *Imagined Communities: Reflections on the Origins and Spread of Nationalism* London: Verso.

Anderson, C. (2006) *The Long Tail: How Endless Choice is Creating Unlimited Demand* London: Random House Business Books.

Arthur, C.J. (2002) *New Dialectic and Marx's Capital* London: Brill.

Baber, Z. (1996) *The Science of Empire: Scientific Knowledge, Civilization and Colonial Rule in India* New York: State University of New York Press.

Bachrach, P., Baratz, M.S. (1970) *Power and Poverty: Theory and Practice* Oxford: Oxford University Press.

Bacon, F. (1905) *The Philosophical Works of Francis Bacon* J.M. Robertson (ed.) London: Routledge.

Banton, M. (1986) *Racial Theories* Cambridge: Cambridge University Press.

Bauchspies, W.K., Croissant, J., Restivo, S. (2006) *Science, Technology and Society: A Sociological Approach* Oxford: Blackwell.

Baxter, H. (1987) "System and lifeworld in Habermas's theory of communicative action", in *Theory & Society* 16(1): 39–86.

Bazin, A. (1967) *What is Cinema? Volume 1* Berkeley: University of California Press.

BBFC (2006) "Research to improve understanding of what players enjoy in video games and to explain their preferences for particular games" London: BBFC.

Bell, H. (1894) *Railway Policy in India* London: Rivington Percival.

Benjamin, W. (1968) "On the work of art in the age of mechanical reproduction", in Arendt, H. (ed.) *Illuminations* New York: Schocken.

Benjamin, W. (1985) *The Origin of German Tragic Drama* London: Verso.

Berger, J. (1974) *Ways of Seeing* Harmondsworth: Penguin.

Berger, P.L., Luckmann, T. (1976) *The Social Construction of Reality: A Treatise in the Sociology of Knowledge* Harmondsworth: Penguin.

Berman, M. (1982) *All That is Solid Melts Into Air: The Experience of Modernity* London: Verso.

Bernal, M. (1987) *Black Athena: On the Afro-asiatic Roots of Civilization* New Jersey: Rutgers University Press.

Bernstein, R.J. (1991) *The New Constellation* Cambridge: Polity Press.

Bijker, W., Hughes, T.P., Pinch, T. (1989) *The Social Construction of Technological Systems: New Directions in the Sociology and History of Technology* London: MIT Press.

Bijker, W. (1997) *Of Bicycles, Bakelites and Bulbs: Toward a Theory of Sociotechnical Change* London: MIT Press.

Bijker, W., Pinch, T. (2002) "SCOT answers, other questions: A reply to Nick Clayton", *Technology & Culture* pp. 361–9.

Bloor, D. (1976) *Knowledge and Social Imagery* Chicago: University of Chicago Press.

Bock, K. (1978) "Theories of progress, development, evolution", in Bottomore, T., Nisbet, R. (eds) *A History of Sociological Analysis* London: Heinemann.

Boggs, C. (1976) *Gramsci's Marxism* London: Pluto Press.

Boghossian, P. (2006) *Fear of Knowledge: Against Relativism and Constructivism* Oxford: Oxford University Press.

Bogost, I. (2006) *Unit Operations: An Approach to Video Game Criticism* London: MIT Press.

Boorstin, D. (1985) *The Discoverers: A History of Man's Search to Know His World and Himself* New York: Vintage Books.

Borgmann, A. (1984) *Technology and the Character of Contemporary Life: A Philosophical Inquiry* London: University of Chicago Press.

Borgmann, A. (1999) *Holding Onto Reality: The Nature of Information at the Millennium* London: University of Chicago Press.

Braverman, H. (1974) *Labour and Monopoly Capital* New York: Monthly Review Press.

Brenner, J., Ramas, M. (1984) "Re-thinking women's oppression", *New Left Review* 144: 33–71.

Bury, J.D. (1920) *The Idea of Progress* London: Dover Books.

Caillois, R. (1958) *Man, Play and Games* Chicago: Illinois University Press.

Capcom (2002) *Resident Evil* (Gamecube).

Castells, M. (1996) *The Information Age: Economy, Society and Culture Volume One: The Rise of the Network Society* Oxford: Blackwell.

Ceruzzi, P. (2000) *A History of Modern Computing* Cambridge Massachusetts: MIT Press.

Clayton, N. (2002) "SCOT: does it answer?" *Technology and Culture* 43: 351–60.

Cockburn, C. (2003) "The material of male power", in MacKenzie, D., Wacjman, J. (eds) *The Social Shaping of Technology* Maidenhead: Open University Press.

Cohen, G.A. (1978) *Karl Marx's Theory of History: A Defence* Oxford: Clarendon Press.

Condorcet, (1980) *Sketch for a Historical Picture of the Progress of the Human Mind* New York: Hyperion Press.

Crary, J. (1993) *Techniques of the Observer: On Vision and Modernity in the Nineteenth Century* London: MIT Press.

Cubitt, S. (2000) *Digital Aesthetics* London: Sage Press.

Curtis, E.K. (1996) "Brush with destiny: A social history of the toothbrush", *Contact Point* 76(2) Summer: 9–11.

Darley, A. (2000) *Visual Digital Culture: Surface Play and Spectacle in New Media Genres* London: Routledge.

Davidson, D. (1984) "On the very idea of a conceptual scheme", in *Inquiries into Truth and Interpretation* Oxford: Clarendon Press.

Davidson, D. (2005a) "The folly of trying to define truth", in *Truth, Language and History: Philosophical Essays* Oxford: Clarendon Press.

Davidson, D. (2005b) "Thinking causes", in *Truth, Language and History: Philosophical Essays* Oxford: Clarendon Press.

Dewey, J. (1997) *Experience and Nature* Chicago: Open Court.

Dews, P. (1987) *Logics of Disintegration: Post-structuralist Thought and the Claims of Critical Theory* London: Verso.

Dibbell, J. (1993) "Rape in Cyber-space", in *Village Voice* 21st December.

Dijksterhuis, E.J. (1961) *The Mechanisation of the World Picture* Oxford: Oxford University Press.

Durkheim, E. (1964) *The Division of Labour in Society* London: The Free Press.

Dyrberg, T.B. (1997) *The Circular Structure of Power* London: Verso.

Eckersley, R. (1990) "Habermas and Green Political Thought: Two roads diverging", *Theory & Society* 19(6): 739–76.

Economist (2006) "Fuzzy maths" Vol 379, No 8477, 13th May.

Economist (2007) "The end of the cash era" Vol 382, No 8516, 17th February.

Edwards, P.N. (1995) "From 'impact' to social process: computers in society and culture", in Jasanoff, G. *et al.* (eds) *Handbook of Science and Technology Studies* London: Sage.

Eisenstein, E. (1983) *The Printing Revolution in Early Modern Europe* Cambridge: Cambridge University Press.

Ellul, J. (1964) *The Technological Society* London: Vintage.

Elster, J. (1985) *Explaining Technical Change* Cambridge: Cambridge University Press.

Elster, J. (1986) *Making Sense of Marx* Cambridge: Cambridge University Press.

Epperson, B. (2002) "Does SCOT answer? A comment", *Technology and Culture* 43: 371–3.

Espiner, T. (2005) "Experts call for global bio-metrics agency", ZDNet UK news 21st October, at *http://news.zdnet.co.uk/* Last accessed 2 February 2007.

Evnine, S. (1991) *Donald Davidson* Cambridge: Polity Press.

Federici, S. (ed.) (1995) *Enduring Western Civilization: The Construction of the Concept of Western Civilization and its "Others"* London: Praeger.

Feenberg, A. (1991) *Critical Theory of Technology* Oxford: Oxford University Press.

Feenberg, A. (1999) *Questioning Technology* London: Routledge.

Feenberg, A. (2000) "Constructivism and technology critique: Replies to critics", *Inquiry* 43: 225–38.

Feenberg, A. (2002) *Transforming Technology: A Critical Theory Revisited* Oxford: Oxford University Press.

Feenberg, A. (2003) "Democratic rationalisation: Technology, power and freedom", in Scharf, R., Dusek, V. (eds) *Philosophy of Technology* Oxford: Blackwell.

Feenberg, A. (2005) *Heidegger and Marcuse: Catastrophe and the Redemption of History* London: Routledge.

Fichman, M. (1993) *Science, Technology and Society: A Historical Perspective* Iowa: Kendall Hunt.

Firestone, S. (1984) *The Dialectic of Sex* London: The Women's Press.

Fitter, M. (1979) "Towards more 'natural' interactive systems", *International Journal of Man-Machine Studies* 11: 339–50.

Focillon, H. (1992) *The Life of Forms in Art* London: Zone Books.

Fortunati, L. (2002) "Italy: Stereotypes, true and false", in Katz, J.E., Aakhus, M. (eds) *Perpetual Contact: Mobile Communication: Private Talk, Public Performance* Cambridge: Cambridge University Press.

Foucault, M. (1980) *Power/Knowledge* Gordon, C. (ed.) New York: Pantheon.

Foucault, M. (1985) *Madness and Civilization* London: Tavistock.

Foucault, M. (1986) *The Birth of the Clinic* London: Routledge.

Freiberger, P., Swaine, M. (1984) *Fire in the Valley: The Making of the Personal Computer* Berkeley California: McGraw-Hill.

Funk, J. (2001) "Children and violent video games: Are there high-risk players?", at *http://culturalpolicy.uchicago.edu/conf2001/papers/funk1.html* Last accessed May 2006.

Galloway, A.R. (2006) *Gaming: Essays on Algorithmic Culture* Minneapolis: University of Minnesota Press.

Game Freak, Incorp. (2007) *Pokemon Diamond/Pearl* Nintendo DS.

Garfinkel, S. (1999) *Database Nation: The Death of Privacy in the Twenty-First Century* Sebastopol: O'Reilly Associates.

Gerovitch, S. (2000) "Striving for optimal control: Soviet cyberneticists as a science of government", in Levin, M.R. (ed.) *Cultures of Control* Amsterdam: Harwood Academic Publishers.

Gershenfeld, N. (2005) *FAB: The Coming Revolution on your Desktop – From Personal Computers to Personal Fabrication* New York: Basic Books.

Gieryn, T. (1999) *Cultural Boundaries of Science: Credibility on the Line* Chicago: University of Chicago Press.

Goggin, G., Newell, C. (2003) *The Social Construction of Disability in New Media* London: Rowman and Littlefield.

Gorz, A. (1980) *Farewell to the Working Class: An Essay in Post-Industrial Socialism* London: Pluto Press.

Gottlieb, N. (2003) "Language, representation and power", in Gottlieb, N., McLelland, M. (eds) *Japanese Cybercultures* London: Routledge.

Gramsci, A. (1985) *Selections From Prison Notebooks* London: Lawrence & Wishart.

Grau, O. (2000) *Virtual Art* London: MIT Press.

Gray, J. (1998) *False Dawn: The Delusions of Global Capitalism* London: Granta.

Green, N., Smith, S. (2004) "A spy in your pocket? The regulation of mobile phone data in the UK", *Surveillance & Society* 1(4): 573–87.

Greider, T. (1997) *One World Ready or Not* London: Allen Lane.

Habermas, J. (1979) "History and evolution", *Telos* 39, Spring: 45–61.

Habermas, J. (1987) *Toward a Rational Society* Cambridge: Polity Press.

Habermas, J. (1989) *Structural Transformation of the Public Sphere* Cambridge: Polity Press.

Habermas, J. (1995) *The Theory of Communicative Action Volume 2: The Critique of Functionalist Reason* Cambridge: Polity Press.

Hacking, I. (1999) *The Social Construction of What?* London: Harvard University Press.

Haraway, D. (1997) *Modest_Witness@Second_Millenium. FemaleMan©_ Meets_OncoMouse™ Feminism and Technoscience* London: Routledge.

Haraway, D. (2000) "A cyborg manifesto: Science, technology and feminism in the 21st century", in Bell, D., Kennedy, B. (eds) *The Cybercultures Reader* London: Routledge.

Harre, R., Gillett, G. (1994) *The Discursive Mind* London: Sage.

Hartmann, H. (1993) "The unhappy marriage of marxism and feminism", in Jaggar, A., Rothenberg, P. (eds) *Feminist Frameworks* Boston: McGraw-Hill.

Hawthorn, G. (1995) *Plausible Worlds: Possibility and Understanding in History and the Social Sciences* Cambridge: Cambridge University Press.

Hayles, N.K. (1999) *How We Became Post-human: Virtual Bodies in Cybernetics, Literature and Informatics* London: University of Chicago Press.

Headrick, D. (1981) *The Tools of Empire: Technology and European Imperialism in the Nineteenth Century* Oxford: Oxford University Press.

Heidegger, M. (2004) "The question concerning technology", in Scharf, R., Dusek, V. (eds) *Philosophy of Technology* Oxford: Blackwell.

Hickman, L. (2001) *Philosophical Tools for Technological Culture: Putting Pragmatism to Work* Indiana: Indiana University Press.

Himanen, P. (2002) *The Hacker Ethic and the Spirit of the Information Age* London: Secker & Warburg.

Hobsbawm, E. (1999) *Industry and Empire* Harmondsworth: Penguin.

Horkheimer, M. (1974) *Eclipse of Reason* New York: Continuum.

Huizinga, J. (1950) *Homo Ludens: A Study of the Play Element in Culture* Boston: Beacon Press.

Ihde, D. (1990) *Technology and the Lifeworld: From Garden to Earth* Bloomington: Indiana University Press.

Ihde, D. (1991) *Instrumental Reason: The Interface Between Philosophy of Science and Philosophy of Technology* Bloomington: Indiana University Press.

Ihde, D. (1993) *Philosophy of Technology: An Introduction* New York: Paragon House.

Introna, L., Nissenbaum, H. (2000) "Shaping the web: Why the politics of search engines matters", *Information Society* 16(3): 169–85.

Jansen, M. (2002) *The Making of Modern Japan* London: Viking.

Jardine, L., Stewart, A. (1999) *Hostage to Fortune: The Troubled Life of Francis Bacon* London: Hill and Wang.

Johnson, J. (1991) "Habermas on strategic and communicative action", *Political Theory* 19(2): 181–201.

Johnson, S. (1997) *Interface Culture: How New Technology Changes the Way We Create and Communicate* San Francisco: Basic Books.

Jordan, T. (2002) *Activism!* London: Reaktion Books.

Juul, J. (2005) *Half Real: Video Games Between Real Rules and Fictional Worlds* Cambridge: MIT Press.

Kant, I. (1961) *The Critique of Judgement* Oxford: Clarendon Press.

Kant, I. (1993) *Critique of Practical Reason* New York: Macmillan.

Kasesniemi, E-L., Rautiainen, P. (2002) "Mobile culture of children and teenagers in Finland", in Katz, J.E., Aarhus, M. (eds) *Perpetual Contact* Cambridge: Cambridge University Press.

Kerr, A. (2006) *The Business and Culture of Digital Games: Gamework/Gameplay* London: Sage.

King, G., Krzywinska, T. (2006) *Tomb-Raiders and Space Invaders* London: IB Tauris.

Kirby, L. (1997) *Parallel Tracks: The Railroad and Silent Cinema* Durham: Duke University Press.

Kirsch, J., Mitchell, D. (2004) "The nature of things: Dead labour, non-human actors and the persistence of Marxism", *Antipode* 36(4): 687–705.

Kirkpatrick, G. (2004) *Critical Technology: A Social Theory of Personal Computing* Aldershot: Ashgate.

Kirkpatrick, G. (2007) "Meritums, spectrums and narrative memories of 'pre-virtual' computing in cold war Europe", *Sociological Review* 55(2): 227–50.

Kline, S., Dyer-Witherford, N., de Peuter, G. (2003) *Digital Play: The Interaction of Technology, Culture and Marketing* London: McGill Queens University Press.

Konami (1998) *Metal Gear Solid* Sony Corporation/Microsoft.

Kuhn, T. (1970) *The Structure of Scientific Revolutions* Chicago: University of Chicago Press.

Kumar, K. (1995) *From Post-industrial to Post-modern Society: New Theories of the Contemporary World* Oxford: Blackwell.

Laclau, E. (1977) *Politics and Ideology in Marxist Theory* London: Verso.

Laclau, E., Mouffe, C. (1985) *Hegemony and Socialist Strategy* London: Verso.

Landes, D.S. (1983) *Revolution in Time: Clocks and the Making of the Modern World* Harvard: Belknap Press.

Lash, S. (2002) *Critique of Information* London: Sage.

Latham, R., Sassen, S. (eds) (2005) *Digital Formations* Princeton: Princeton University Press.

Latour, B. (1993) *We Have Never Been Modern* Harvard: Harvard University Press.

Latour, B. (2005) *Re-Assembling the Social: An Introduction to ANT* Oxford: Oxford University Press.

Laurel, B. (1993) *Computers as Theatre* Reading, MA: Addison-Wesley.

Law, J., Hassard, J. (1999) *Actor Network Theory and After* Oxford: Blackwell.

Lean, T. (2004) "What would I do with a computer? The shaping of the Sinclair computer 1980–86", unpublished MA thesis, University of Sheffield, cited by kind permission.

Levathes, L. (1994) *When China Ruled the Seas: The Treasure Fleet of the Dragon Throne 1405–1433* Oxford: Oxford University Press.

Levy, S. (1984) *Hackers: Heroes of the Computer Revolution* Harmonds-worth: Penguin.

Leyshon, A., French, S., Thrift, N., Crewe, L., Webb, P. (2003) "Accounting for e-commerce: abstractions, virtualism and the cultural circuit of capital", *Economy & Society* 34(3): 428–50.

Lindberg, D.C. (1976) *Theories of Vision from Al Kindi to Kepler* Chicago: University of Chicago Press.

Lukes, S. (2005) *Power: A Radical View* Basingstoke: Palgrave-Macmillan.

MacKenzie, D. (1991) *Inventing Accuracy: A Historical Sociology of Nuclear Missile Guidance Systems* London: MIT Press.

Malik, K. (1996) *The Meaning of Race* New York: New York University Press.

Maravall, J.A. (1986) *Culture of the Baroque: Analysis of a Historical Structure The History of Literature Volume 25* Manchester: Manchester University Press.

Marcuse, H. (1964) *One Dimensional Man* London: Routledge.

Markoff, J. (2006) *What the Dormouse Said* London: Viking.

Marx, G. (2003) "Some information age techno-fallacies", *Journal of Contingencies and Crisis Management* 11(1), March: 25–31.

Marx, K., Engels, F. (1967) *Manifesto of the Communist Party* Harmondsworth: Penguin.

Marx, K. (1972) *A Contribution to the Critique of Political Economy* London: Lawrence & Wishart.

Marx, K. (1982) *The German Ideology* London: Lawrence & Wishart.

Marx, K. (1983) *Capital Volume 1* Moscow: Progress Publishers.

Marx, K. (1981) *Grundrisse* Harmondsworth: Penguin.

May, C. (2002) *The Information Society: A Sceptical View* Cambridge: Polity Press.

Mayr, O. (1986) *Authority, Liberty and Automatic Machinery in Early Modern Europe* London: Johns Hopkins University Press.

McGinn, C. (1982) *The Character of Mind* Oxford: Oxford University Press.

Mead, G.H. (1967) *Mind, Self and Society: From the Standpoint of a Social Behaviourist* Chicago: University of Chicago Press.

Meek, R. (ed.) (1973) *Turgot on Progress, Sociology and Economics* Cambridge: Cambridge University Press.

Meikle, S. (1985) *Essentialism in the thought of Karl Marx* Oxford: Duckworth.

Mellor, M. (1997) *Feminism and Ecology* Cambridge: Polity Press.

Melucci, A. (1996) *The Playing Self: Person and Meaning in Planetary Society* Cambridge: Cambridge University Press.

Misa, T.J., Brey, P., Feenberg, A. (eds) (2003) *Modernity and Technology* London: MIT Press.

Misa, T.J. (2004) *Leonardo to the Internet: Technology and Culture from the Renaissance to the Present* London: Johns Hopkins University Press.

Moody, G. (2002) *Rebel Code: Linux and the Open Source Revolution* London: Penguin.

Mueller-Vollmer, K. (ed.) (1994) *The Hermeneutics Reader* London: Continuum.

Mumford, L. (1947) *Technics and Civilization* London: Routledge.

Myerson, G. (2001) *Heidegger, Habermas and the Mobile Phone* Cambridge: Icon.

Ndalianis, A. (2003) *Neo-Baroque Aesthetics and Contemporary Entertainment* London: MIT Press.

Negroponte, N. (1995) *Being Digital* London: Coronet.

Newman, J. (2004) *Videogames* London: Routledge.

Nickerson, R.S. (1976) "On conversational interaction with computers", in *Proceedings of the ACM/SIGGRAPH Workshop October 14th–15th* Pittsburgh.

Noble, D. (1984) *Forces of Production: A Social History of Industrial Automation* New York: Knopf Press.

Norman, D.A., Draper, S.W. (1986) *User-centred System Design: New Perspectives Human-Computer Interaction* London: Laurence Erlbaum Associates.

Pacey, A. (1991) *Technology in World Civilization* London: MIT Press.

Pacey, A. (1999) *Meaning in Technology* London: MIT Press.

Paine, C. (dir.) (2006) *Who Killed the Electric Car?* Sony Pictures Classics.

Paine, S. (2006) "The human centrifuge", *New Scientist* 4th November.

Panter-Brick, C., Layton, R.H., Rowley-Conwy, P. (eds) (2001) *Hunter-Gatherers: An Interdisciplinary Perspective* Cambridge: Cambridge University Press.

Parker, R. (1986) *The Subversive Stitch: Embroidery and the Making of the Feminine* London: The Women's Press.

Peirce, C.S. (1998) *Essential Writings* New York: Prometheus Books.

Pinker, S. (1994) *The Language Instinct* Harmondsworth: Penguin.

Poster, M. (1995) *The Second Media Age* Cambridge: Polity Press.

Poster, M. (2006) *Information Please* London: Duke University Press.

Postman, N. (1993) *Technopoly: The Surrender of Culture to Technology* New York: Vintage Books.

Ranger, T. (1992) "The invention of tradition in colonial Africa", in Hobsbawm, E. Ranger, T. (eds) *The Invention of Tradition* Cambridge: Cambridge University Press pp. 211–62.

Ratto, M. (2005) "Embedded technical expression: Code and the leveraging of functionality", *The Information Society* 21: 205–13.

Raymond, E. (1999) *The Cathedral and the Bazaar: Musings on Linux and Open Source by an Accidental Revolutionary* California: O'Reilly & Associates.

Rheingold, H. (2000) *The Virtual Community: Homesteading on the Electronic Frontier* London: MIT Press.

Rosenthal, J. (1998) *The Myth of Dialectics: Reinterpreting the Marx-Hegel Relation* London: Macmillan.

Roszack, T. (1968) *The Making of a Counter-Culture: Reflections on the Technocratic Society and Its Youthful Opposition* London: Faber and Faber.

Rousseau, J-J. (1984) *A Discourse on Inequality* Harmondsworth: Penguin.

Ryan, M-L. (2001) *Narrative as Virtual Reality: Immersion and interactivity in literature and electronic media* Baltimore: Johns Hopkins University Press.

Saisselin, R.G. (1992) *Enlightenment Against Baroque: Economics and Aesthetics in the Eighteenth Century* London: University of California Press.

Sassen, S. (2006) *Territory, Authority, Rights: From Medieval to Global Assemblages* Princeton: Princeton University Press.

Science Museum of Minnesota (2006) "Museum of questionable medical devices", at *http://www.geocities.com/bayou/museumquack.html* Last accessed May 2007.

Selwyn, N. (2002) "Learning to Love the Micro: The discursive construction of "educational" computing in the UK 1979–89", *British Journal of Sociology of Education* 23(3): 427–43.

Selwyn, N. (2003) " 'Doing IT for the kids': re-examining children, computers and the 'information society' ", *Media, Culture & Society* 25: 351–78.

Shields, R. (2003) *The Virtual* London: Routledge.

Sismondo, S. (2004) *An Introduction to Science and Technology Studies* Oxford: Blackwell.

Skinner, Q. (1992) *The Foundations of Modern Political Thought Volume 1: The Renaissance* Cambridge: Cambridge University Press.

Smith, D. (2006) *Globalisation: The Hidden Agenda* Cambridge: Polity Press.

Spacewar (2005) "Secret codes in printers may allow government tracking", at *http://www.spacewar.com/news/cyberwar-05zzf.html* Last accessed 14 September 2006.

Spacewar (2006) "Computer hacker group offers stealth internet surfing", at *http://www.spacewar.com/reports/Computer_Hacker_Group_Offers_Stealth_Internet_Surfing_999.html* Last accessed 3 October 2006.

Stafford, B. (1994) *Artful Science: Enlightenment Entertainment and the Eclipse of Visual Education* London: MIT Press.

Stallabrass, J. (1996) *Gargantua: Manufactured Mass Culture* London: Verso.

Stump, D. (2000) "Socially Constructed Technology", *Inquiry* 43: 217–24.

Strydom, P. (1992) "The onto-genetic fallacy: The immanent critique of Habermas's developmental-logical theory of evolution", *Theory, Culture & Society* 9(3): 65–93.

Taylor, P.A. (1999) *Hackers: Crime in the Digital Sublime* London: Routledge.

Thompson, J.B. (1995) *The Media and Modernity* Cambridge: Polity Press.

Thomson, I. (2000a) "From the question concerning technology to the quest for a democratic technology: Heidegger, Marcuse, Feenberg", *Inquiry* 43: 203–16.

Thomson, I. (2000b) "What's wrong with being a technological essentialist? A response to Feenberg", *Inquiry* 43: 429–44.

Thrift, N. (2006) "Re-inventing invention: New tendencies in capitalist commodification", *Economy & Society* 35(2): 279–306.

Tsivian, Y. (ed) (2004) *Lines of Resistance: The Cinema of Dziga Vertov* Sacile: Le Giornato del Cinema Munto.

Turkle, S. (1984) *The Second Self: Computers and the Human Spirit* London: Granada.

Turkle, S. (1995) *Life on the Screen: Identity in the Age of the Internet* London: Weidenfeld and Nicholson.

Turner, F. (2006) *From Counterculture to Cyberculture: Stewart Brand, the Whole Earth Network and the Rise of Digital Utopianism* Chicago: University of Chicago Press.

Urry, J. (2000) *Sociology Beyond Societies* London: Routledge.

Valve Software (1998) *Half Life* London: EA/Sierra Games.

Wacjman, J. (2004) *Techno-feminism* Cambridge: Polity Press.

Walvin, J. (1992) *Black Ivory: A History of British Slavery* London: Fontana Press.

Weber, M. (1974) *The Protestant Ethic and the Spirit of Capitalism* London: Unwin University Books.

Wikipedia (2007) Entry for "FaceBook", at *http://en.wikipedia.org/wiki/Facebook#_note-informer* Last accessed July 2007.

Winner, L. (1980) "Do artefacts have politics?", *Daedelus* 109: 121–36.

Winner, L. (1993) "Social constructivism: Opening the black box and finding it empty", in MacKenzie and Wacjman (eds) *The Social Shaping of Technology* Maidenhead: Open University Press.

Index